HOT CARS
HEAD TO HEAD
THE WORLD'S BEST AUTOMOBILES COMPARED

General Editor: James Peene

BARNES & NOBLE

NEW YORK

Editorial and design by
Amber Books Ltd

Project Editor: James Bennett
Design: EQ Media

Picture Credits:
Images © Aerospace/Art-Tech and IMP/Art-Tech

ISBN-13: 978-0-7607-8975-9
ISBN-10: 0-7607-8975-4

Printed and bound in Singapore

1 3 5 7 9 10 8 6 4 2

Contents

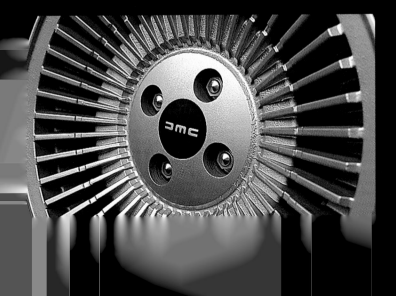

Introduction

Can you imagine the joy at being asked to edit a book comparing and contrasting some of the world's greatest cars? It's every serious auto buff's dream to be given a platform to wax lyrical about what they like or don't like about a particular brand, model or type of car. That's not because we want to force our opinions on anyone else until they come round to our way of thinking, but simply because we care passionately about something which some less imaginative souls than ourselves regard as nothing more than a means of getting from A to B.

How terrible it would be if the world's motor manufacturers took the same view. If they did, there would be no Ferrari Testarossa, Porsche 911, or Jaguar E-Type to covet, and legendary names like Lamborghini would be known for producing nothing more evocative than tractors. The world would certainly be a duller place.

Catching sight of a great-looking car, or perhaps your childhood fantasy or current dream automobile, can brighten up even the dullest journey and become a talking point when you meet another like-minded soul at the other end of it. And what serious car lover hasn't found themselves embroiled in a heated "discussion" about the particular merits or otherwise of a car with their coworkers, family, or friends?

Pitting some of the most revered names in automotive history against one another and comparing speed, acceleration, handling, and many other attributes besides, in this book we pose some of those age-old questions: Which is the most desirable, the Corvette Sting Ray or Jaguar E-type? Which is the more refined, a Cadillac or Mercedes? Or which is the faster, the Dodge Viper or AC Cobra?

Accompanied by some fantastic studio and archive photographs, and an array of statistics and specs, we've attempted to answer all these questions and many, many more, evaluating some of the most celebrated, desirable, and expensive automobiles ever produced.

James Peene

Classic Battles

It's often difficult to appreciate fully the diverse range of shapes, styles, and construction methods adopted by car manufacturers over the years. Produced in the days before wind tunnels and computers dictated how a car should look, each of the cars in this chapter is as different as the next. In fact, you can spot the difference between an E-type and Corvette Sting Ray at 100 paces, and a trained ar can even tell which one is which when sitting in them blindfolded. That's because, as capable and well-rounded as the vast majority of contemporary cars are, they lack the extra something special that these classics have by the barrelful: soul. Truly great cars have to arouse passion and ignite your senses, and that's something each and everyone of these has the power to do.

Built before penny-pinching committees and the cost of fuel made sports cars impractical, the gas-guzzling muscle cars of the '60s and '70s just wouldn't be made under today's rules and regulations, so we're lucky our ancestors built them for us. Because these cars were so unfettered and uncompromising, competition between muscle car manufacturers generated fierce rivalry, and spawned some truly fantastic machines, as you'll discover in this chapter.

You'll discover a diverse collection of V8, flat-six, water, and air-cooled engines, mounted amidships, in the back, or up front, and all of it encased in bodywork sculpted in the golden age of motoring, when muscle cars, pony cars, and no-holds-barred racetrack refugees rubbed shoulders as they fought for supremacy.

Jaguar E-TYPE

The E-type created a sensation on both sides of the Atlantic when it appeared in 1961. It was a hot-seller in the US, and Chevrolet's response two years later was an all-new Corvette, the Sting Ray. Could that match the Jaguar?

Sleek, sporty, and elegant the Jaguar E-type is the ultimate automotive icon. It came to symbolize London in the swinging sixties, and is still widely regarded as the most beautiful road car ever produced.

With looks and handling that were way ahead of its time, the E-type is more advanced than the Corvette, and this shines through on the road. So, while the Chevrolet's less sophisticated underpinnings mean it struggles to cope on bumpy, uneven surfaces, the Jaguar's fully-independent suspension, with longer travel and softer springing, means it takes them in its stride. The Corvette's stiffer underpinnings

also make it feel skittish and more of a handful when driving at speed, while the Jaguar feels more poised and relaxed by comparison. In addition, the E-type is also more of a grand tourer than a small sports coupe, so feels the more refined of the two on longer journeys.

While it is true that the E-type's power-assisted disc brakes feel a bit inadequate by today's standards, they're still a world away from the drums mounted on all four corners of pre-1965 Corvettes. Which, in a car capable of speeds as high as 240km/h (150mph) – the Corvette will reach a marginally less impressive 217km/h (135mph) – is an important safety feature, and a crucial ingredient which inspires the confidence to drive it fast.

JAGUAR E-TYPE

Engine Capacity	3769cc (230ci)
Weight	1117kg (2463lb)
Power	198kW (265bhp)
Torque	352.5Nm (260lb-ft) @ 4000 rpm
Price	$3400
Acceleration:	
0–30mph (48km/h)	2.9 sec.
0–60mph (96km/h)	7.3 sec.
0–90mph (145km/h)	16.2 sec.
Standing ¼ mile (400m)	15.1 sec.
Maximum Speed	240km/h (150mph)

Chevrolet CORVETTE STING RAY

CHEVROLET CORVETTE STING RAY

Engine Capacity	5358cc (327ci)
Weight	1428kg (3150lb)
Power	268kW (360bhp)
Torque	447.4Nm (330lb-ft) @ 3000 rpm
Price	$4252
Acceleration:	
0–30mph (48km/h)	3.1 sec.
0–60mph (96km/h)	6.7 sec.
0–90mph (145km/h)	14.5 sec.
Standing ¼ mile (400m)	14.2 sec.
Maximum Speed	217km/h (135mph)

With its razor sharp styling the Corvette is as iconic to many as the E-type and is proof, if any were needed, that 1960s America had the know-how to build a car to rival anything Europe could produce.

The E-type might feel more refined than the Corvette, but whether that is a positive is a matter of personal opinion. Chevrolet designed the 'Vette to have a characteristically hard and jarring ride. They did this because they believed this is what their customers expected of a muscle car – and its more macho image appeals to a different sort of driver. While Jaguar went for technical innovation, Chevrolet opted to keep things as simple as possible. Basic and cheap-to-produce underpinnings and a big-block engine give the Corvette a rawer edge. Jab the throttle at any speed and it will kick you in the back and surge forward accordingly. If you like your sports cars to feel brutal and capable of giving you a fright from time to time, the Corvette will more than deliver.

Wilder it may be, but the Corvette has arguably the better interior of the two. It's more spacious, with wider seats, more generous legroom, and its flashier, jukebox-inspired dashboard gives it a real, home-grown all-American feel.

Jaguar E-TYPE

Inside Story

Experience with the Le Mans-conquering racing D-types was put to good use. Jaguar's new E-type had a similarly advanced monocoque center-section chassis with a tubular front section to carry the engine. Even better than that is the superb independent rear suspension with its four springs and shocks. Front suspension is by double wishbones and longitudinal torsion bars, steering by rack and pinion, and disc brakes are fitted all around.

POWER PACK

The E-type has a 3.8-liter development of the classic XK engine, first seen in 1948 in Jaguar's postwar XK120 in 3.4-liter form. It is a long-stroke, in-line six-cylinder with iron block and alloy head, twin chain-driven overhead camshafts and two inclined valves per cylinder. It is heavy but powerful, tuneable and very strong, as proved by its numerous racing successes in the Ferrari-beating C- and D-types.

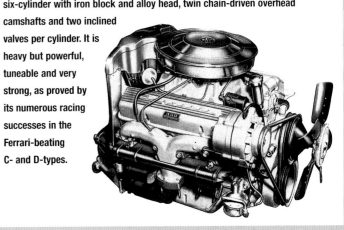

Ride

Longer suspension travel and softer springing means a better, more forgiving ride in the E-Type. All Corvettes have a characteristic rock hard ride — all part of its "muscular" appeal.

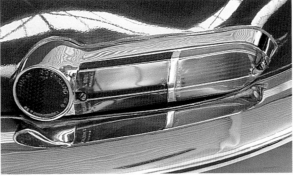

Braking

The all-round discs of the E-type are not as good as today's systems, but are still far in advance of the Corvette's fade-prone drums. You needed the optional sintered metal drum linings to begin to cope with the Sting Ray's performance. Whereas Jaguar had used discs all around since 1957, Chevrolet did not offer them until 1965.

Chevrolet CORVETTE STING RAY

Inside Story

A massive steel chassis holds a striking fiberglass body in open or closed forms. Under that lies independent rear suspension for the first time in a Corvette. It is a far simpler system than the E-type's, using radius and control arms and a transverse leaf spring. Front suspension is by double wishbones, steering by recirculating ball, and four large drum brakes do the stopping. Discs were not available until 1965. Wheels are steel or optional alloy.

POWER PACK

The specs of the Corvette V8 sound basic but the engine is impressive. It is all cast-iron with just one camshaft, operating two in-line valves per cylinder via hydraulic lifters. It is a compact unit with a short stroke (825mm/3.25 in). When Chevrolet added optional Rochester fuel injection, output rose to 268kW (360bhp) – more than 45W per cc (1bhp per cubic inch) of displacement, which was an amazing specific power output for the time.

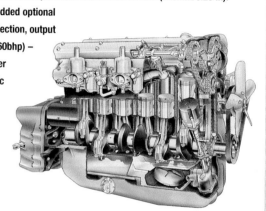

Performance

Outstanding for the time and very little to choose between the two. The E-type is quicker off the line, is caught by 96km/h (60mph), but holds its own to 146km/h (100mph) before the greater power and torque of the Corvette really makes itself felt.

Road holding

The E-type's better chassis and advanced suspension give it the edge on anything but really smooth surfaces, but the Corvette puts more rubber on the road with its larger tires. Both originally wore crossply tires, which offer much more levels of grip than modern radials, but are more predictable.

Porsche 356

This is a test between a traditional heavy and powerful front-engine, rear-drive car, and a lightweight, compact rear-engine model. Could the last of the XK line hold its own against the Carrera 2 in the vital American market?

The 356's appearance may have earned it the nickname the "little bath-tub", but one thing the first generation Porker never did was handle like one. This iconic machine is the car that forged Porsche's reputation, became a design classic, and created a legacy still traceable in today's high-powered 911s.

Shunning the traditional approach to building sports cars, Porsche opted for an unconventional layout that resulted in an aircooled flat-four engine hung out behind the rear axle. All that weight at the back means the 356 has fantastic traction but is trickier to drive on the limit than the XK150. You need total commitment to drive it fast. Lift off in a corner, especially in the wet, and the Jaguar may forgive you, but

the Porsche can bite the unwary driver as a pendulum effect will come into force and result in a spin.

Experienced drivers with cat-like reflexes can control a tail-happy Porsche with careful inputs of throttle, but its love-it-or-loathe it handling has caught many less skilled drivers out.

With just four-cylinders and only 1996cc (120cu in) to play with the 356 loses out on power to the XK150, but makes up for it by being both lighter and more aerodynamic, so its slippery shape and clever design easily compensates for what it lacks in out and out grunt.

PORSCHE 356

Engine Capacity	1966cc (120cu in)
Weight	1140kg (2513lb)
Power	115kW (155bhp)
Torque	177.6Nm (131lb-ft) @ 4600 rpm
Price	$7595

Acceleration:

0–30mph (48km/h)	3.3 sec.
0–60mph (96km/h)	9.4 sec.
0–90mph (145km/h)	23.0 sec.
Standing ¼ mile (400m)	16.9 sec.
Maximum Speed	196km/h (122mph)

Jaguar XK150

JAGUAR XK150

Engine Capacity	3442cc (210cu in)
Weight	1449kg (3194lb)
Power	157kW (210bhp)
Torque	292.9Nm (216lb-ft) @ 3000 rpm
Price	$5150
Acceleration:	
0–30mph (48km/h)	2.8 sec.
0–60mph (96km/h)	8.7 sec.
0–90mph (145km/h)	21.5 sec.
Standing ¼ mile (400m)	16.9 sec.
Maximum Speed	217km/h (135mph)

Unlike the light and nimble Porsche, the heavyweight XK150 was designed to handle predictably and appeal to the more affluent 1950s motorist. While Porsche went for a "less is more" approach, Jaguar opted to lavish as much chrome, leather, and wood on its opulent flagship as possible.

All those trinkets look good but add weight, so Jaguar compensated by fitting a large-capacity engine up front which kicked out a healthy 3442cc (210cu in). Both cars will cover the ¼ mile (400m) in 16.9 seconds, but the Jaguar will

do it with less effort from its water-cooled twin-cam engine and has an overdrive fitted to make cruising more relaxed than the higher-revving aircooled Porsche.

Look beneath the XK150's sleek, heavily sculpted bodywork and you'll find convention rules the day. Porsche opted for a single monocoque construction, while Jaguar built a huge separate chassis onto which it bolted an old-as-the-hills live axle set-up. Behind its narrow wheels and skinny tires, race-proven four-wheel disk brakes bring everything to a halt again.

Jaguar produced the XK for 13 years, until the E-type was ready. The XK150 is the ultimate incarnation of the breed and was always fast and great value for money.

Porsche 365

Inside Story

In concept, the Carrera's layout is still that of the VW Beetle. Its flat-four engine hangs over the rear beyond the four-speed transmission. The chassis consists of a pressed-steel floorpan carrying trailing arm and torsion bar front suspension, and swing axles at the back with transverse torsion bars. Three body styles were available: Cabriolet, Coupe and, the most famous, Speedster. A GT Coupe model had lightweight Speedster seats, perspex windows and some alloy panels.

POWER PACK

Early flat-four Carrera engines had a roller bearing crankshaft, but for the Carrera 2, it is conventional with plain bearings that have a longer life expectancy. The four overhead cams are still driven by a complicated system of four shafts and no less than 13 bevel gears. It is a high-revving, short stroke (9 x 7cm/3.62 x 2.91in) design and produces its excellent 177Nm (131lb-ft) maximum torque high up the rev band at 4600 rpm.

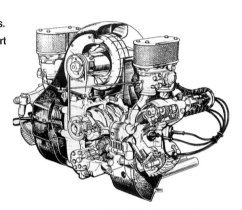

Accommodation

The XK's leather interior doesn't hold you in place through corners. Its Moss transmission is awkward and the big steering wheel is a necessity for slow-speed turns. The Porsche interior is more businesslike, featuring adjustable seats, light steering and an easy gear shifting.

Handling

Oversteer was an inescapable part of driving the Carrera 2. It helped the car turn in sharply to corners so the Porsche was more nimble than the XK. The XK was well balanced, and nothing like its weight suggests. Its steering is quick enough to catch the back end when it slides out.

Jaguar XK150

Inside Story

Tradition reigned here, with a massive separate chassis and a live rear axle located and supported by semi-elliptic leaf springs. The XK150 was modern in having servo-assisted Dunlop disc brakes all around, just like the racing D-types. Overdrive operating on the top two gears gave the XK driver a total of six gears. Independent front suspension was by wishbones, sprung by longitudinal torsion bars. An anti-roll bar was also installed.

P O W E R   P A C K

The famous XK iron-block, alloy head, twin-cam, straight-six is used in 3442-cc (210cu in) form with 8cm (3.26in) bore and 11cm (4.17in) stroke. It produces 292Nm (216lb-ft) at 3000 rpm of torque to go with the 157kW (210bhp) output. The 150S had triple carburetors and an outstanding power output of 188kW (265bhp), giving a 0–96.5km/h (0–60mph) time of 7.6 seconds.

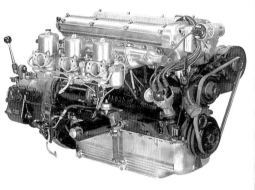

Performance

Both cars cover ¼ mile (400m) in 16.9 seconds, but the XK gets off the line faster. It's also a couple of seconds quicker to 160km/h (100mph). The Carrera driver has to work his engine hard and exploit the flat-four's rpm to keep up with the torquier XK, which has a better power-to-weight ratio.

Braking

The race-proven Dunlop disks on the XK helped the heavyweight Jaguar shed speed effortlessly. The lighter Carrera was an easier proposition to brake. By April 1962, Porsche had its own design of "ring"-type disk brakes, but they couldn't match the Dunlops and were soon replaced with conventional ATE disks.

Porsche 911S

Porsche paid considerable attention to every aspect of the 911S and it is an exhilarating performer. The Alpine A110 was developed primarily for competition, and is an enthusiast's delight. But which is the best car?

Porsche has always believed that racing improves the breed, and nowhere is this approach to building cars more visible than in the 911S. The highly-tuned version of the evergreen 911 became an instant success in endurance racing and rallying, and is widely regarded as one of the purest expressions of the model.

The Alpine A110 might ooze aggression from every angle and look as though it was built with the sole intention of winning races, but the 911 exudes a simple and refined, elegance that belies its sporting potential. With a high compression version of the standard models' flat-six, the 911S has a good 29kW (40bhp) more than the Renault and still manages to feel smoother and more refined to drive.

The Porsche is also the more civilized machine of the two, and even though both cabins feel narrow, if you had to pick one for a long cross-country journey, it would be the 911. It is roomier, lighter, and airier and its more passenger-friendly cabin is arguably better built, too.

One of the best things about the 911 is that owners could take it to the track, race all weekend, climb back in it and drive to work again on the Monday morning, which is something you certainly couldn't, or wouldn't, want to do in an Alpine.

PORSCHE 911S

Engine Capacity	1991cc (121cu in)
Weight	1030kg (2271lb)
Power	119kW (160bhp)
Torque	195.2Nm (144lb-ft) @ 5200 rpm
Price	$7255
Acceleration:	
0–30mph (48km/h)	3.9 sec.
0–60mph (96km/h)	7.4 sec.
0–90mph (145km/h)	24.3 sec.
Standing ¼ mile (400m)	16.1 sec.
Maximum Speed	225km/h (140mph)

Renault A110

RENAULT A110

Engine Capacity	1296cc (79cu in)
Weight	600kg (1323lb)
Power	89kW (120bhp)
Torque	122Nm (90lb-ft) @ 4500 rpm
Price	$6168
Acceleration:	
0–30mph (48km/h)	2.5 sec.
0–60mph (96km/h)	6.3 sec.
0–90mph (145km/h)	18.2 sec.
Standing ¼ mile (400m)	15.0 sec.
Maximum Speed	215km/h (134mph)

Widely considered to be one of the strongest rally cars of all time, the pug-like Alpine was built to be racing car first and road car second. So, depending on your point of view, this is either its greatest asset or biggest weakness.

Both the A110 and 911 have large-capacity engines to give them a sting in the tail so the best advice to the driver of either car would be to handle them with extreme care, especially when near the limit, but the Alpine feels the more aggressive and animal-like of the two, so will appeal more to the competition-minded driver.

Its tubular chassis and fiberglass body mean the A110 is lighter and more delicately balanced than the Porsche, yet still requires a precise touch and experienced head to get the most of it. With its lower center of gravity and minimal weight it feels the most secure in corners and changes direction quicker, so the sense of speed and handling are more acute.

Small, capable, and built for speed, the Alpine is ultimately flawed. More of a rally weapon than something to be used on the road, as capable of winning races as it obviously is, the Alpine is just too extreme and uncompromising, but its wild ride is something to take pleasure in all the same.

Porsche 911S

Inside Story

The 911S is the high-performance version of the 911 which was launched three years after the base model. To cope with the extra power, the independent suspension (wishbones and torsion bars up front, semi-trailing arms and torsion bars at the rear) is beefed up and includes Koni shocks and a rear anti-roll bar. It has vented disk brakes, and wider alloy wheels replaced the steel ones. In 1968 the wheelbase was stretched to improve roadholding.

POWER PACK

Porsche's classic air-cooled flat-six engine is a legend. The all-alloy unit is hung out behind the rear wheels just like a VW Beetle. It sounds terrific and has many racing-style touches like dry-sump lubrication. The S version of the 2.0-liter unit has twin Weber carburetors and a higher compression ratio for a power output of 119kW (160 bhp). This increased to 134kW (180bhp) when the engine was bored out to 2.2 liters in 1969.

Accommodation

The Alpine is so narrow inside there is hardly room for two side by side. Alongside it, the Porsche feels spacious and quite luxurious, with more comfortable seating, more space and better trim.

Road holding

Despite the tail-happy handling at extreme speed, both cars have surprisingly tenacious grip until that point. Undoubtedly, the Porsche has the better grip from its wider tires and lets go more progressively than the flighty Alpine, but the Alpine's negative rear camber and low center of gravity give it fine traction.

Inside Story

Alpine founder Jean Redélé's approach was to use Renault parts in his own setting. As such, the A110 has a simple lightweight tubular backbone chassis fitted with components taken from the Renault 8 Gordini (and later the Renault 16). There are two shocks for each rear wheel, and the 1300-engined models are fitted with a five-speed transmission. The bodywork is molded from fiberglass, in order to keep weight low. A front-mounted fuel tank helps balance out the rear weight bias.

POWER PACK

While Alpine was Renault's race and rally star, Gordini was its engine wizard. The A110 1300 engine is based on the unit used in the Renault 8 Gordini. In Alpine form it is bored out to 1296cc (79cu in) which, combined with its two twin-choke Weber carburetors, develops a solid 88kW (120bhp). To reach this high power level it has to rev very hard, up to a screaming 7200 rpm.

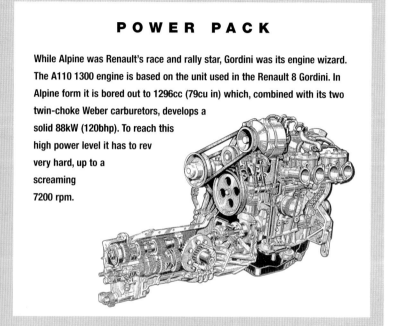

Performance

When one car has a 2.0-liter engine and the other a 1.3-liter unit, it is no surprise that the one with the bigger engine wins, but the contest is closer than you may imagine. In terms of top speed, the Porsche is marginally in front, but the Alpine sprints away a little faster from the line. The Porsche has less peaky delivery, making it much more agreeable for everyday driving.

Handling

The best advice when you are driving both these cars is "handle with care". It takes time to learn how to deal with rear-engined cars. Both offer good grip, but the lighter Alpine changes direction more assertively.

MGB

The MGB and Fiat 124 Spider are two quintessential European sports cars of the late 1960s and the 1970s. Both have sporty styling and an attractive price, but which offers the most performance and fun for the money?

Twisty European roads were made for compact two-seat roadsters, so it's hardly surprising that Britain's best-selling sports car of all time is the small and ubiquitous MGB.

Launched in 1962 and marketed as "The Great British Sports Car", the MGB relied on simple, tried-and-tested mechanicals to get the job done and keep prices low, whereas the Fiat was built using state-of-the-art technology, with more complex suspension and disk brakes both front and back. As a result, there was more to go wrong with it and consequently the Spider cost a good deal more to produce and buy than the mechanically mundane but equally fun MG.

Although the MG lacks a rear seat, the one in the Fiat isn't really usable, so interior space is much the same in both cars. Of the two, the MG has more character and oozes period charm, so what it lacks in handling and performance, it makes up for with personality.

The Fiat feels more exotic and interesting than the MGB, but there lies the problem. It could prove itself to be a little too temperamental or brittle, and that's why it was comfortably outsold by the rugged, down-to-earth MGB.

MGB

Engine Capacity	1798cc (110cu in)
Weight	1107kg (2442lb)
Power	71kW (95bhp)
Torque	150.5Nm (111lb-ft) @ 3000 rpm
Price	$2670

Acceleration:

0–30mph (48km/h)	3.6 sec.
0–60mph (96km/h)	11.0 sec.
Standing ¼ mile (400m)	17.9 sec.
Maximum Speed	169km/h (105mph)

FIAT 124 SPIDER

FIAT 124 SPIDER

Engine Capacity	1608cc (98cu in)
Weight	995kg (2193lb)
Power	73kW (98bhp)
Torque	128.8Nm (95lb-ft) @ 4200 rpm
Price	$3181

Acceleration:

0–30mph (48km/h)	3.8 sec.
0–60mph (96km/h)	10.5 sec.
Standing ¼ mile (400m)	17.5 sec.
Maximum speed	180km/h (112mph)

If the MGB is traditionally British, then the Fiat 124 is quintessentially Italian. Although it appears to be similar to the rival roadster on paper, in the metal the Spider actually feels more chic and sophisticated. Always a strong seller on both sides of the Atlantic, the 124 has the distinction of being the longest-running and most successful sporting Fiat ever produced, yet in terms of exclusivity and desirability it has the more common MG beat.

The Spider is also the more forgiving machine to drive at speed. Both cars have less than perfect live rear axles, but you need to concentrate slightly harder in the MG than the

Fiat, and corners have to be taken with more caution. With its lighter rack and pinion steering the MG also feels vaguer than the more 'chuckable' Spider in twists and turns, and body roll is also less pronounced in the Fiat. Mechanically speaking, the Spider's live axle is better located than that in the MG, so it digs in when starting to turn and hugs the road better.

Both engines make the right kind of sports car noises, but the MGB's B-series engine can trace its roots back to 1953 so feels more dated and less willing to rev than the peppy double overhead-cam unit in the sportier-feeling Spider.

23

MGB

Inside Story

Compared to the old MGs that made the marque so popular in the USA, the MGB was a modern car, with a unitary body and wind-up windows. Underneath, however, it is more traditional with the good old B-series engine, a live rear axle suspended on semi-elliptic springs, front lever-arm shock absorbers and wishbones. The front brakes are disks and the rear ones drums. Later cars have an improved rear axle and a fully synchromeshed transmission.

P O W E R   P A C K

The origins of the British Motor Corporation B-series engine can be traced back to 1953, when it was launched in 1.5-liter form. A straightforward four-cylinder unit, it has cast-iron construction, overhead valves and three main bearings. For use in the MGB it is bored out to 1.8 liters. This unit has a lot more torque than the previous versions, although not much more power: 70kW (95bhp) in European cars and just 40kW (55bhp) in US versions.

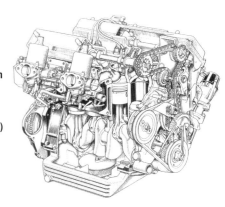

Ride

With live rear axles, the ride on both cars is not particularly impressive. Despite having its rear axle suspended by older style elliptical leaf springs, the MGB is more composed than the Spider on smooth roads. It also offers a sportier feel, which is reminiscent of a true sports car.

Accommodation

Both cars have spacious interiors for sports cars, although the MGB has more generous cabin space. The Fiat has a padded rear seat, but offers very little legroom. The MGB has more classic dials and an attractive console.

Fiat 124 Spider

Inside Story

The drop-top sports Fiat is based on the 124 sedan, but with rear- instead of front-wheel drive. It has four-wheel disk brakes and a rigid rear axle, suspended by coil springs and located by a Panhard rod and twin radius arms. The front end consists of coil springs and wishbones. Due to its more sporty design, the Spider uses servo-assisted brakes and a five-speed manual transmission on US-spec cars. These suspension and brake improvements in 1969 made the car even more enjoyable.

POWER PACK

Fiat is an acknowledged master of the overhead-cam engine. The 124 Spider, which was fitted with a classic DOHC 1.4-liter unit, was launched in 1966 and produces a healthy 66kW (90bhp). This engine continued in production until 1972. In 1969 it was joined by a longer-stroke 1608cc (98cu in) unit with an extra 6kW (8bhp), and in 1972 came a 1756cc (107cu in) development with up to 87kW (118bhp). The final evolution of this engine was a 2.0-liter in 1979.

Road holding

The Fiat wins in the road-holding stakes thanks to its superior rear suspension and better body control. It will grip through bends where minor bumps can unsettle the MGB. A lower center of gravity is an advantage in the Italian car.

Braking

There is no question that the advanced (for the time) four-wheel power brakes of the Fiat inspire more confidence. The MGB has front disk brakes but rear drums and takes slightly longer to come to a halt. If they are not servo-assisted brakes, the brakes tend to lock up more easily.

Ferrari 250 TR

As the ultimate in front-engined 1950s sports-racing cars, the Ferrari 250 Testarossa and the Jaguar D-type beg to be compared, even though they weren't exact contemporaries and rarely competed against each other on the track.

They certainly don't build racing cars like this anymore. In fact the 250 TR, or Testarossa ("red head") is the second-most valuable Ferrari ever produced, after the 250 GTO. In fact, it would set you back about $8,000,000 if you could find one for sale today, which is a staggering increase over the $11,500 it would have cost when it was new.

Both machines are truly stunning to look at, but unlike today's crop of Formula One cars, are completely individual and each has its own unique style. The Jaguar is a work of aerodynamic art and looks like it's traveling at

top speed even when standing still, but there's something about the Ferrari's sculpted curves and elegant lines that give it the edge over the Jaguar. As a scarlet, racing Italian it has a mystique and aura about it that the more workmanlike D-type can't compete with, and by comparison the Jag looks like one of the also-rans making up the numbers on the grid.

If they were to line up side by side on a racetrack the Ferrari would most likely take the honours as well, being faster to 190km/h (120mph), and 30km/h (18mph) quicker than Jaguar going flat out.

FERRARI 250 TR

Engine Capacity	2953cc (180cu in)
Weight	748kg (1649lb)
Power	220kW (300bhp)
Torque	340.3Nm (251lb-ft) @ 5500 rpm
Price	$11,500
Acceleration:	
0–30mph (48km/h)	2.8 sec.
0–60mph (96km/h)	6.0 sec.
0–90mph (145km/h)	19.0 sec.
Standing ¼ mile (400m)	13.8 sec.
Maximum Speed	286km/h (178mph)

Jaguar D-TYPE

JAGUAR D-TYPE

Engine Capacity	3442cc (210cu in)
Weight	1011kg (2231lb)
Power	184kW (250bhp)
Torque	328.1Nm (242lb-ft) @ 4000 rpm
Price	$9875

Acceleration:

0–30mph (48km/h)	2.4 sec.
0–60mph (96km/h)	5.4 sec.
0–90mph (145km/h)	21.0 sec.
Standing ¼ mile (400m)	14.0 sec.
Maximum Speed	257km/h (160mph)

It's a pity these cars never had the chance to compete against each other on the racetrack, because it would have made for a truly breathtaking spectacle. Both machines racked up some incredible victories in their time, with the Ferrari dominating the 3-liter class of the 1958 World Sports Car Championship, while the D-type showed its mettle by winning the grueling Le Mans 24 Hours an amazing three times.

If you dared take either one of these cars on the circuit today, the chances are you'd be too nervous of breaking them to consider using either to their full potential, but it would be a close run thing if you did.

The Ferrari is ultimately faster, but the Jaguar is quicker to accelerate, so would give the Ferrari a run for its money on a twisty circuit with shorter straights, because with a skilled driver at the wheel it would eat into any lead the Ferrari might build up over the longer sections by being able to brake later into the corners. It wouldn't just be a matter of having to hold your nerves in the less skittish D-type either, because the British offering is equipped with more efficient Dunlop disk brakes, which have more bite and are less prone to fade than the Italian's cruder finned drums.

Ferrari 250 TR

Inside Story

There are two types of Testarossa: one built for customers that has a conventional live rear axle, and the factory cars with a more sophisticated de Dion axle. Some later factory cars also came equipped with rear-mounted transaxles to cure nose-heaviness. The chassis is similar to the old four-cylinder Testarossa, Although longer and stronger, it uses similar coil-sprung front suspension. Finned drum brakes are fitted both front and rear.

POWER PACK

The Testarossa's 60-degree V12 engine develops 220kW (300bhp) and has a capacity of just under 3.0 liters to keep within the limit for championship endurance racing in 1958.

Testarossa means "red head" in Italian and took its name from the crackle-red finish on the engine's camshaft covers. Ferrari opted to use this single camshaft per bank engine, also found in the 250 GT road cars, to keep maintenance relatively simple for private owners as well as for reliability on the track.

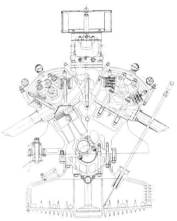

Accommodation

Functional efficiency is the main concern in both cars. The dash of the Ferrari, with its elliptical five-dial binnacle, is perhaps more visually appealing than that of the Jaguar, which is more rudimentary with classic Smith gauges set in leatherette. Embracing bucket seats are a feature of both cars.

Performance

Lighter and more powerful than the D-type, the Testarossa just has the edge through the gears, reaching 160km/h (100mph) in 16 seconds. Both cars have torquey, flexible engines, but the Ferrari has a better transmission.

Jaguar D-TYPE

Inside Story

The D-type features an aluminum monocoque tub, which provides exceptional stiffness while keeping weight to a minimum. By 1950s standards the D-type boasted cutting-edge engineering, including four-wheel Dunlop disk brakes – before they appeared on a production road car – and a radius arm rear suspension with a transverse torsion bar, although a live rear axle is retained. The front suspension is fairly conventional and consists of upper and lower wishbones with twin torsion bars.

POWER PACK

In the D-type, Jaguar's versatile twin-cam straight-six engine is equipped with dry-sump lubrication – to combat oil surge on corners – and breathes through three dual-choke Weber carburetors. Later factory cars feature experimental fuel injection, which boosts power from 184–202kW (250–275bhp). A stiff engine, with an iron block and seven main-bearing crankshaft, the XK unit powered Jaguar road cars until the mid-1980s.

Ride

Both cars have a fairly stiff and skittish road ride as they were set up for smooth, fast circuits like Le Mans. Factory Testarossas with de Dion suspension are slightly better than the D-type.

Braking

With Dunlop power brakes, the D-type shows a decisive advantage over the Ferrari, which uses traditional large, finned drums. Disk brakes do not suffer from fade like drums and they also offer a powerful response. The 250's drums do have good cooling, because of the shape of the fenders.

Oldsmobile 4-4-2

Pontiac's GTO was the original muscle car, but by 1966 others had jumped on the bandwagon. The Oldsmobile 4-4-2 was among the most roadable Detroiters of its time, but how does it measure up to the "Great One"?

Newton's third law states that for every action there is an equal and opposite reaction. So, envious of the success its major competitor was enjoying with the GTO, Oldsmobile rushed its own muscle car into production, creating the 4-4-2 to swell its coffers.

Some claim that it was Olds and not Pontiac that created the first muscle car when it shoehorned a V8 into its 88 series back in 1949, but it wasn't until the 4-4-2 of 1964 that it did it again, and the consensus is that Pontiac got there first. However, coming second doesn't make it second best. The 4-4-2 got its name from its 4-speed manual transmission,

4-barrel carburetor and 2 exhausts, and is a fantastic street machine for tearing up the highway while searching for some illicit drag-racing.

Both cars are capable of tripping the timing lights at highly illegal speeds, although when you get to a corner you'd be better off in the Olds than in the GTO as it has the more supple and assured suspension, with a better balanced and poised feel, despite both machines having pretty much the same chassis and underpinnings. These cars are so remarkably similar that choosing a preference is often a case of brand loyalty or personal taste.

OLDSMOBILE

4 - 4 - 2

Engine Capacity	6555cc (400cu in)
Weight	1633kg (3600lb)
Power	268kW (360bhp)
Torque	596.6Nm (440lb-ft) @ 3600 rpm
Price	$3500

Acceleration:

0–30mph (48km/h)	3.0 sec.
0–60mph (96km/h)	6.8 sec.
Standing ¼ mile (400m)	14.7 sec.
Maximum speed	200km/h (125mph)

Pontiac GTO

PONTIAC GTO

Engine Capacity	6374cc (389cu in)
Weight	1792kg (3950lb)
Power	268kW (360 bhp)
Torque	574.9Nm (424lb-ft) @ 3600 rpm
Price	$3600

Acceleration:

0–30mph (48km/h)	2.9 sec.
0–60mph (96km/h)	6.2 sec.
Standing ¼ mile (400m)	14.1 sec.
Maximum speed	200km/h (125mph)

Designed to be a street, rather than track, performer, the GTO was a smart idea implemented at the right time. While other manufacturers were concentrating on their larger models, Pontiac shrewdly dropped its big block V8 into a smaller, cheaper car it believed boy racers would snap up like hot cakes.

Considered by many to be America's first true muscle car, the GTO was engineered specifically to appeal to the new generation of performance-minded car buyers, who were also about to be offered the Ford Mustang. It was brash,

stylish and extremely quick in its day and by contemporary standards, even if the name was a bugbear to some purists, being "inspired" by the legendary Ferrari 250 GT.

Clearly this is a car that offers plenty of performance and thrills for the money. And with its nose-down stance, like a drag racer, and massively torquey 6374cc (389cu in) V8 engine, it certainly doesn't disappoint.

Despite having a smaller capacity motor than the Oldsmobile, the GTO has triple-barrelled carburetors, the same top speed, and is marginally quicker lower down. Performance-wise there's so little to separate them, choosing one is purely a matter of preference. Do you go for the original and first, or one of its many capable imitators?

Oldsmobile 4-4-2

Inside Story

An optional package on the body-on-frame, mid-size, two-door Olds Cutlass coupe and convertible, the 4-4-2 includes revised spring and shock rates, plus a larger front and the addition of a rear anti-roll bar. This results in road performance that was much better than most muscle cars of its day, not to mention possibly the best balanced, too. Braking technology is still way behind though, with four-wheel drum brakes.

POWER PACK

In 1964, the first year of the 4-4-2, the largest engine offered was a 5408cc (330-cu in) V8 with 231kW (310bhp). The following year, a 6554cc (400-cu in) V8 became standard, and for 1966 an optional three-/two-barrel carburetor setup was offered on this engine, plus a W30 fresh-air induction courtesy of flexible tubes running from openings in the front bumper to the air cleaner. The V8 thumps out a more than respectable 268kW (360 bhp) and 596Nm (440lb-ft) of torque.

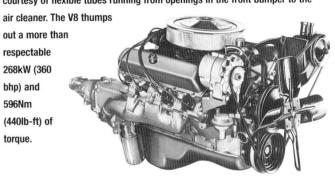

Road holding

Both cars have essentially the same chassis and running gear, but their performance becomes notably different on twisty roads. The GTO has a greater tendency to understeer and loses grip more easily at high speeds. The Olds has better suspension geometry and, combined with both front and rear anti-roll bars, has a more balanced feel and poise.

Ride

Compared to contemporary European sporty cars, both vehicles have a comparatively soft ride. Interestingly, the Oldsmobile has a more supple ride, yet at the same time is far more at home carving corners than the mighty Pontiac.

Inside Story

For 1966, the GTO and the Tempest, on which it was based, got a larger, curvier body, although fluted taillights were a GTO exclusive. Underneath, it is much the same as the 4-4-2 with a separate body and chassis, plus all-coil-sprung suspension and a live rear axle. GTOs could be specified with a Positraction limited-slip differential and rear gearing from 3.08:1 to 4.33:1. Although similar to the Olds, the GTO is less adept at corner carving due, in part, to its chassis tuning and single anti-roll bar.

POWER PACK

The original concept of the GTO was to stick the big-car V8 in the mid-size Tempest. By the time the Goat became its own model, the V8 still displaced 6374cc (389cu in), but power was up to 246kW (335bhp) with a Carter four-barrel carburetor and 265kW (360bhp) with the optional Tri-Power. This was fitted to 19,045 cars before GM outlawed multi-carb layouts midway through 1966. It is an equal match for the Olds 400 unit.

Performance

With its Tri-Power carb setup, the GTO boasts more horsepower and rockets to 96.5km/h (60mph) in just 6.2 seconds. For this year only, Olds also offers triple two-barrels. The GTO goes through the ¼-mile (400m) traps in just 14.15 seconds at 158km/h (98.5mph), but the Olds comes second with 14.7 seconds at 156km/h (97mph).

Accommodation

Although they are both two-door cars, the 4-4-2 and GTO offer adequate room to seat five adults in comfort, but the front seats are not the most supportive. Both cars have full gauges plus a central console with a floor shifter. Because Oldsmobile caters to a more affluent audience, its cabin is more user friendly.

Oldsmobile 4-4-2

One of the most revered muscle cars of all time, the 1969 Dodge Charger R/T is certainly among the quickest. But how does it fare against the formidable 1970 Oldsmobile 4-4-2 W-30, which brought race technology to the street?

While Dodge bided its time before joining the muscle car party, Oldsmobile jumped in the moment it saw how lucrative the new market was. The car it came up with was the 4-4-2, but it doesn't feel like a rush-job when you drive one today.

With its four-barrel carburetor, four-speed manual transmission and twin exhausts, the Oldsmobile is one of the best-balanced muscle cars ever, and was always a few steps ahead of its Detroit competition.

Both cars have gargantuan engines in the nose and feel front heavy, but the Oldsmobile deals with it better thanks to its

more sophisticated and heavy-duty suspension, and the use of front and rear anti-roll bars. Even at full speed and considering its size and weight, the 4-4-2 feels surprisingly controllable through twists and turns and is more assured than the Charger. In fact, cornering is one of the Oldsmobile's particular strong points. Its wide tires have plenty of grip and tons of bite, body lean is much less pronounced than you might expect, and it can be flung into corners with less care than the Dodge.

A heck of a lot of car for the money, the Oldsmobile was less brash than many of its competitors and still feels like the more gentlemanly choice.

OLDSMOBILE 4-4-2

Engine Capacity	7456cc (455cu in)
Weight	1684kg (3713lb)
Power	276kW (370bhp)
Torque	574.9Nm (500lb-ft) @ 3600 rpm
Price	$3376
Acceleration:	
0–30mph (48km/h)	2.4 sec.
0–60mph (96km/h)	6.2 sec.
0–90mph (145km/h)	14.3 sec.
Standing ¼ mile (400m)	14.1 sec.
Maximum Speed	212km/h (132mph)

Dodge Charger R/T

DODGE CHARGER R/T

Engine Capacity	6980cc (426cu in)
Weight	1654kg (3646lb)
Power	317kW (425bhp)
Torque	664Nm (490lb-ft) @ 3200 rpm
Price	$3592

Acceleration:

0–30mph (48km/h)	2.1 sec.
0–60mph (96km/h)	5.5 sec.
0–90mph (145km/h)	14.0 sec.
Standing ¼ mile (400m)	13.9 sec.
Maximum speed	212km/h (132mph)

The Dodge Charger was a response to the fastback craze began by the Ford Mustang and Plymouth Barracuda. Having waited to throw its hat into the ring until it had a machine worthy of the muscle car tag, and which wouldn't draw sales away from Chrysler's other divisions, the mean-looking Charger was based on the Coronet platform and became an instant sales success.

Even today it is regarded as being one of the definitive muscle cars, and you don't need a degree in engineering to understand why. The Dodge isn't that technically advanced and is certainly less sophisticated than the Oldsmobile, but,

as the saying goes, there's no substitute for cubic capacity, and the Charger has that by the boatload. R/T stands for Road and Track and indicates that any car wearing such a badge is the high performance version, so it goes without saying that the Charger is rapid: faster to 160km/h (100mph) than the 4-4-2, and only conceding 3km/h (2mph) when both are traveling at full tilt.

With such a heavy engine (57% of the Charger's weight is at the front), it has a tendency to skate across the road at speed and dive under braking, but Coke-bottle curves were "in" for the second generation Charger and when it looks this good, you can forgive it almost anything.

Oldsmobile 4-4-2

Inside Story

Also built off an intermediate platform, in this case the A-body Oldsmobile Cutlass, the 4-4-2 has a separate steel perimeter chassis and all-coil-sprung suspension. Items unique to the 4-4-2 include stiffer springs and Delco shock absorbers, plus standard front and rear stabilizer bars. The live rear axle came with standard 3.91:1 gearing, but optional ratios up to 5.00:1 could be specified. The W-30 option added a number of extras – plastic front inner fenders and an aluminum differential housing.

POWER PACK

In 1970, General Motors removed the 6555cc (400cu in) limit on its mid-size muscle cars. All 4-4-2s came standard with 7456cc (455cu in) in engines this year. This cast-iron mill has a stock 10.5:1 compression ratio and was rated at 268kW (365bhp) in base form. Ordering the W-30 package got a fully balanced and blueprinted engine, plus an aluminum intake, bigger air filter and forced air induction – good for 272kW (370bhp).

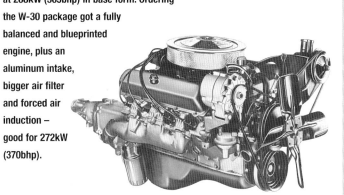

Accommodation

Inside, the R/T and 4-4-2 both offer seating for four and sporty appointments. The Oldsmobile, however, exudes greater quality and refinement, plus its front bucket seats offer better lateral support than the Charger's flatter seats. The 4-4-2's small-diameter, fat-rimmed steering wheel is more sporty and easier to grip, too.

Road holding

Although both cars are decidedly nose-heavy, the Charger skates across the road if too much power is applied. The Oldsmobile, by comparison, has a more sophisticated suspension, with both front and rear anti-roll bars, and more responsive steering. It holds the line better and is much easier to control and correct if oversteer results.

Dodge Charger R/T

Inside Story

Part of Chrysler's B-body family of intermediates, the 1969 Charger R/T rides a 297cm (117in) unitary chassis. The front suspension uses longitudinal torsion bars instead of coil springs, while at the rear there is a live Dana axle with a Sure-Grip differential mounted on semi-elliptic multi-leaf springs. A variety of axle ratios up to 4.10:1 were offered, and although four-wheel drum brakes were standard on R/Ts, front disks were a welcomed option.

POWER PACK

Although base Chargers were fitted with a 5211cc (318cu in) V8, the performance-oriented R/T model was offered with only two engines. The top performer is the awesome 6980cc (426cu in) Hemi, so named because of the shape of its combustion chambers. In 1969, street Hemi specifications read like this: forged-steel crank and connecting rods, high-lift camshaft and a dual-plane intake with twin Carter AFB four-barrel carburetors.

Performance

The Charger's engine displacement may be 475cc (29cu in) less, but the awesome Hemi V8 produces more power (312 versus 272kW/425bhp versus 370bhp). In the acceleration stakes, the Charger is the victor, covering the 1/4-mile (400m) in just 13.9 seconds; with the W-30 running through the traps in 14.1.

Ride

Different suspension setups result in a different highway ride. The Charger, with its torsion-bar front springs, does a better job at isolating road shocks and is less tiring to drive on bumpy roads. With its stiffer coil springs and anti-roll bars, the 4-4-2 jolts more alarmingly over potholes.

Chevrolet CAMARO IROC-Z

Camaro-versus-Mustang battles have been raging since 1967, but among the most closely contested of all are those between the IROC-Z and Mustang GT of the late 1980s. Both cars have legions of fans, but which one emerges victorious?

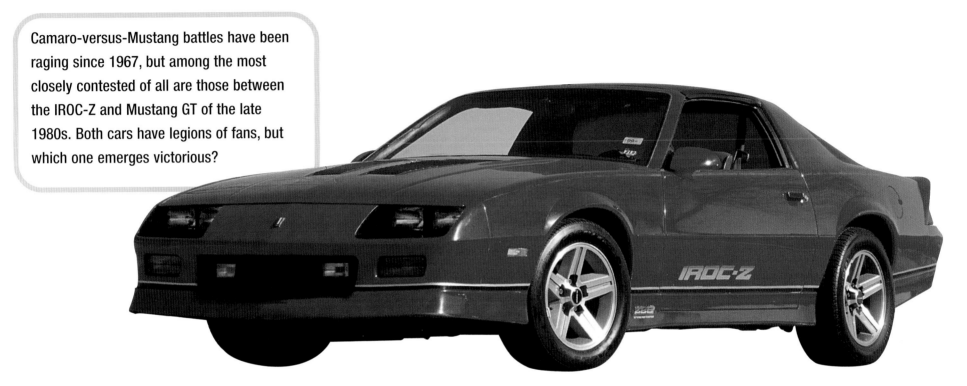

For every snake there's a ladder, and for every Mustang it seems there's a Camaro. These two incredibly potent muscle cars have been vying for supremacy for so long now that anyone who bought one first time around would have found the time to raise teenage children by the time these incarnations hit the streets.

Not that either of these cars could be accused of going through their difficult teenage years. Their looks might have changed a great deal since the first time we saw cars bearing the Mustang or Camaro tag, but they're the same animals at heart and, if anything, are more potent and dangerous than they were in their youth. Certainly the

Camaro in IROC-Z form has used the time to grow into its looks, while the dumpy, ungainly Mustang is now a shadow of its former self.

This third-generation Camaro also packs more punch than the Mustang. Its power pack churns out fractionally less bhp than the Ford's, but still allows it to out-accelerate and rocket on to a higher eventual top speed.

Neither car really does full justice to its illustrious predecessor, but if you forget about their former glories and judge each machine on its own merits, then the Camaro wins this round on all scores.

CHEVROLET CAMARO IROC-Z

Engine Capacity	5.7l (348cu in)
Weight	1583kg (3490lb)
Power	238kW (220bhp)
Torque	433.9Nm (320lb-ft) @ 3200 rpm
Price	$18,179
Acceleration:	
0–30mph (48km/h)	2.3 sec.
0–60mph (96km/h)	6.8 sec.
0–90mph (145km/h)	18.4 sec.
Standing ¼ mile (400m)	14.8 sec.
Maximum Speed	240km/h (149mph)

Ford MUSTANG GT

FORD MUSTANG GT

Engine Capacity	5l (302cu in)
Weight	1483kg (3270lb)
Power	168kW (225bhp)
Torque	406.7Nm (300lb-ft) @ 3000 rpm
Price	$15,548
Acceleration:	
0–30mph (48km/h)	2.3 sec.
0–60mph (96km/h)	6.7 sec.
0–90mph (145km/h)	18.8 sec.
Standing ¼ mile (400m)	14.5 sec.
Maximum Speed	232km/h (144mph)

Old age might have taken its toll on the Mustang's once-handsome looks, but when the GT rejoined the third generation line-up in 1982 a section of the American motoring press declared "the boss is back".

Glance past its arguably dated looks today and you can understand why this sentiment was bandied around. Beneath all those stuck-on spoilers and needless factory options is a pretty fine-handling car that will top out at a whisker short of 235km/h (145mph) and hit 95km/h (60mph) in 6.7 seconds – impressive, even by today's standards.

It's all well and good to read about how a car handles on the limits, but in the real world few cars are ever driven to such extremes, which is why the Mustang possibly beats the Camaro to the finishing line in this department. Sure, its rear end will feel more skittish under rapid cornering, but that just makes it more fun at day-to-day regular speeds, and is the softer, more refined and comfortable machine to drive on proper road surfaces.

At the end of the day both Ford and the buying public were pleased enough with the Mustang GT to keep building and buying it for six years, and while it might have lost this battle, it's still a worthy addition to the Mustang's more hallowed legend.

Chevrolet CAMARO IROC-Z

Inside Story

The Camaro was redesigned and downsized for 1982, with the wheelbase trimmed to 256cm (101in). The front-engined, live rear axle was retained, though MacPherson struts replaced the short/long arms, and the rear got coils in place of leaf springs. IROC-Zs have stiffer spring rates, gas-pressurized Delco shocks and front and rear anti-roll bars for outstanding handling. At the rear, a Panhard rod reduces sideways movement. Braking is by four-wheel disks.

POWER PACK

Named for the International Race of Champions, the IROC-Z was an outgrowth of the hot Z28 and shares its 5.0-liter V8. When it made its debut in 1985, it was fitted with Tuned Port Injection and boasted an impressive 158kW (215bhp). For 1987, Chevy turned up the heat again and made the L98 Corvette engine an option. Packing 213kW (220bhp) from 5.7 liters, it was perfect for 'Stang hunting. As the years progressed, the 5.7-liter engine made as much as 180kW (245bhp).

Road holding

Here, things even up a little. Both cars hold the line well, although the Mustang requires more steering input. With less suspension travel, the Chevy tends to bottom out on rough roads, but on smooth surfaces it feels slightly more secure.

Braking

The Camaro has the edge here, by virtue of its four-wheel disks, larger tires and better proportions. It takes just 48m (159ft) to come to a halt. Although it has front disks, the GT's rear drum are a handicap.

Ford MUSTANG GT

Inside Story

Riding a 255cm (100.4in) wheelbase of the Fox platform, the Mustang also has MacPherson strut front suspension and a live rear axle suspended by coil springs. GTs have stiffer springs to compensate for the weight of the V8 engine and gas-pressurized shocks, with an extra rear pair (horizontally mounted) to quell wheelhop under fierce acceleration. Front and rear anti-roll bars are standard on V8-powered Mustangs, as are 28.5cm (11.25in) power front disk brakes.

POWER PACK

The heart of the GT is the sweet 5.0-liter small-block Windsor V8. It may be a simple pushrod engine, but it is still one of the most effective and potent engines around. Packing 165kW (225bhp) at 4200 rpm, it enables the Mustang to run rings around most of the opposition. Fuel is delivered through a sequential multipoint injection system. From 1989, all Mustang V8s were fitted with a revised air metering system.

Accommodation

Here, it is down to individual preference. The Camaro has a snugger interior, giving the driver a closer-to-the-road feel. The Ford has a more upright driving position but boasts slightly better ergonomics, plus greater leg and luggage space.

Performance

Although it gives away 184cc (50cu in), the GT puts out more power than the IROC-Z, and being both lighter and stiffer, it is quicker through the ¼ mile (400m), with the Camaro a very close second.

Chevrolet CORVAIR CORSA

Chevrolet insisted that it had a Mustang fighter in the beautiful second-generation 1965 Corvair. But can this sporty and unique compact really measure up to the original and favourite pony car?

In 1965 the Corvair was famously singled out for criticism in Ralph Nader's book *Unsafe At Any Speed: The Designed-in Dangers of the American Automobile*, and those words still ring in its ears today.

Whereas the Mustang carved out its own niche, the Corvair was inspired by the flood of foreign imports like the rear-engined Volkswagens it competed against. And, while the Mustang was always a sporty, yet skittish performer in the bends, the Corvair could prove tricky in the corners if you didn't know how to handle it.

With its unequal weight distribution, the Corvair struggles to match the Mustang in terms of handling, but is not as bad as

you might expect, and you may even be surprised at just how far its limits really are. In the right hands, its 63:37 bias towards the rear can be turned into an advantage and help fling it round corners.

A true 132kW (180bhp) from an aircooled engine is not to be sniffed at, and with all that weight to compensate for, the Corvair has a pretty sophisticated front and rear wishbone set-up that would possibly outperform the Mustang – if only the rest of it was a bit more conventional. But, with its slightly softer springing, the Corvair proves the less tiring machine over long distances, so it's the family-friendly choice.

CHEVROLET CORVAIR CORSA

Engine Capacity	2687cc (164cu in)
Weight	1115kg (2460lb)
Power	134kW (180bhp)
Torque	406.7Nm (300lb-ft) @ 2400 rpm
Price	$2608
Acceleration:	
0–30mph (48km/h)	3.5 sec.
0–60mph (96km/h)	10.2 sec.
0–90mph (145km/h)	37.0 sec.
Standing ¼ mile (400m)	18.1 sec.
Maximum Speed	185km/h (115mph)

Ford MUSTANG GT

FORD MUSTANG GT

Engine Capacity	4736cc (289cu in)
Weight	1265kg (2789lb)
Power	156kW (210bhp)
Torque	359.3Nm (265lb-ft) @ 3200 rpm
Price	$2614
Acceleration:	
0–30mph (48km/h)	3.6 sec.
0–60mph (96km/h)	8.9 sec.
0–90mph (145km/h)	27.5 sec.
Standing ¼ mile (400m)	17.0 sec.
Maximum Speed	177km/h (110mph)

While the Corvair never quite shrugged off the stinging critique of its handling, the Mustang reveled in the glowing praise heaped upon it. An overnight sales success that created a legend and took America by storm, it has always stolen the limelight and kept the Chevrolet in the shade.

And why not? It's arguably the better-looking car, with its muscular styling and trademark stallion racing across its front grille; the simpler, perhaps more elegant Corvair just doesn't have the Mustang's looks, so doesn't excite in the same way. The Convair suffered relatively poor sales, while the Mustang became one of the best-selling sports cars of all time.

The Convair is also not as much fun to drive as the Mustang. The racy Ford packs more of a punch with its torquey, front-mounted V8. While it doesn't exactly leave the Corvair in its dust, it will out-accelerate it and is faster than many supposedly more advanced European sports cars in a straight line. Reassuringly, it has good brakes too – front disks, as opposed to the Corvair's weaker drums all round.

The Mustang's stiffer suspension makes it feel the more poised and assured machine of the two when cornering at speed. If someone gave you the chance of a ride in either of these rapid and characterful drop-tops, you would almost certainly choose the Mustang.

Chevrolet CORVAIR CORSA

Inside Story

Debuting for 1960, the Corvair was radical, to say the least. It had unitary body/chassis construction and independent-wishbone front and semi-trailing swing-axle rear suspension. The more advanced second-generation model arrived in 1965. It had a few notable improvements, namely a more sophisticated wishbone-type rear suspension and a stiffer anti-roll bar to give more neutral handling. Adequate four-wheel drum brakes are also fitted.

P O W E R   P A C K

One of the Corvair's most radical features is its air-cooled, flat-six engine. Created under the watchful eye of Edward N. Cole, the motor was a horizontally-opposed unit with an aluminum block and divided crankcase, plus a separate barrel for each cylinder. In 1964, displacement was increased from 2376 to 2687cc (145 to 164cu in). In 1965, it got new cylinder heads, a revised manifold and four progressively linked carburetors. Adding a turbocharger gave 132kW (180bhp).

Handling

Even with a much stiffer suspension, the Mustang is still an inherent understeerer and is not truly content at high-speed cornering. The Corvair, by comparison, is easy to fling around bends. Despite its narrower tires, the more sophisticated suspension set-up makes for a surprisingly neutral, well balanced car.

Road holding

With its front and rear wishbones keeping the wheels level at all times, the Corvair Corsa feels safe, responding smartly to any steering input. Stiffer springs and shocks may help, but the Mustang GT still betrays its origins and can be skittish if too much power is applied.

Ford MUSTANG GT

Inside Story

Although it looks every inch a sporty tourer, underneath the Mustang is essentially a Ford Falcon. Like the Corvair, it has unitary construction, but the similarity ends there. The engine is mounted up front, driving the rear wheels with a live axle held in place by longitudinal leaf springs. The front suspension is all independent with unequal-length wishbones and coil springs. Like the Corvair, the Mustang has standard four-wheel drum brakes, though front discs were available as an option.

POWER PACK

Early Mustangs were powered by a 2786cc (170cu in) six. Most buyers, however, specified V8s. A 4260cc (260cu in) unit with 164bhp was initially the base V8, though this was replaced by a 143/154kW (195/210bhp) 289 after September 1964. These figures were later boosted to 147/165kW (200/225bhp). A Hi-Performance 289 was also offered with 199kW (271bhp) – it had an aggressive high-lift cam, higher-compression heads and an open-element air cleaner.

Performance

Both cars have four-on-the-floor transmissions, though the Mustang, with its greater power and more torque, clearly has the edge. It can sprint to 96km/h (60mph) 1.3 seconds quicker than the Corsa, although it has less traction. The Corvair, despite taking just over 10 seconds to reach 96km/h (60mph), still feels sporty to drive.

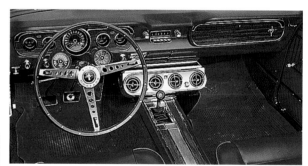

Accommodation

Both cars are essentially 2+2s with their back seats having little room. Though the Corvair has a slight edge in rear seat room, the Mustang's cabin feels more inviting and sporty.

Chevrolet CONFEDERATE

Chevrolet's Confederate series was one of the cleanest-looking cars of its time and also one of the most reliable. In the same year, 1932, rival Ford launched its V8-powered Model 18, but does it really hold an advantage over the Chevy?

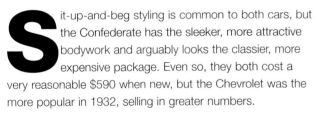

Sit-up-and-beg styling is common to both cars, but the Confederate has the sleeker, more attractive bodywork and arguably looks the classier, more expensive package. Even so, they both cost a very reasonable $590 when new, but the Chevrolet was the more popular in 1932, selling in greater numbers.

With a high center of gravity, solid axles and tall thin wheels, handling is hardly going to be a major consideration here. Both machines will roll alarmingly if you enter into a bend too fast, but it's much less pronounced in the Confederate, which also feels the more refined machine at slower speeds too.

Both cars are decidedly primitive inside and look pretty similar. The difference is that Ford built its cars down to a

cost to keep them affordable, while Chevrolet adopted a less penny-pinching attitude to its products. This is why you'll find better-quality materials and a more welcoming and opulent feel in the Confederate.

Despite being a practical and functional automobile at heart, the Chevrolet pandered more to its owners' comforts and requirements. Thanks to its greater style and higher levels of sophistication it was even dubbed the "baby Cadillac" by those in the know, while the dowdier Ford became famous as an affordable car for the people.

CHEVROLET CONFEDERATE

Engine Capacity	3180cc (194cu in)
Weight	1247kg (2750lb)
Power	44kW (60bhp)
Torque	160Nm (118lb-ft) @ 900 rpm
Price	$590
Acceleration:	
0–10mph (16km/h)	5.8 sec.
0–20mph (32km/h)	11.2 sec.
0–60mph (96km/h)	42.0 sec.
Standing ¼ mile (400m)	46.1 sec.
Maximum Speed	112km/h (70mph)

Ford MODEL 18

more impressive mid-range power and dizzyingly high top speed of 125km/h (78mph) – which is 12km/h (8mph) more than the Chevy can muster.

FORD MODEL 18

Engine Capacity	3621cc (221cu in)
Weight	1083kg (2389lb)
Power	48kW (65bhp)
Torque	176.3Nm (130lb-ft) @ 1250 rpm
Price	$590
Acceleration:	
0–10mph (16km/h)	5.4 sec.
0–20mph (32km/h)	10.8 sec.
0–60mph (96km/h)	41.2 sec.
Standing ¼ mile (400m)	44.7 sec.
Maximum Speed	125km/h (78mph)

Thirties America may have been in the depths of the Great Depression, but there were still plenty of fine automobiles on the market – if, that is, you had the disposable income to afford them. But which to choose? The sleek Confederate or the cheaper Model 18 with its wonderful V8 engine?

Obviously with just 44–48kW (60–65bhp) between them, speed isn't going to be the deciding factor here. Both are slow by modern standards, but the Ford's V8 made a difference when it was new, and buyers were drawn to its

Not that you'll want to travel too quickly in either of these bone-shakers; transverse leaf springs feature heavily on both machines so you'll be in for a bumpy ride. And, you won't want to explore the limits of 1930s brake technology either. The drums are none-too-hot on either machine, but the bitier Confederate has a slight advantage over the Ford.

It didn't have the looks or the sales of the Chevrolet, but the Model 18 was as cheap as Ford could make it, equipped with a V8, and became the definitive 1930s automobile, while only enthusiasts remember the Confederate now.

Chevrolet CONFEDERATE

Inside Story

In the early 1930s, the vast majority of automakers still built separate chassis cars and offered different bodies designed to fit on the same frame. Chevrolet's Confederate series followed conventional thinking with a ladder-type chassis consisting of two main rails with beams welded across it. Its suspension is equally basic, with solid axles used at both front and rear. Springing at the front is controlled by a single, transverse, semi-elliptic leaf with lever-arm shock absorbers. At the back is a semi-floating axle that takes power from the three-speed synchromesh manual transmission through a set of 4.1:1 gears to the 46cm (18in) wheels.

POWER PACK

Under the upright cowling is one of Chevrolet's most durable and longest-running production engines, the "Stovebolt" six. This motor was engineered by Ormond E. Hunt and based on an earlier design. It features a cast-iron block and cylinder head, with slotted head bolts from which the engine received its nickname. By 1932, the three-main-bearing engine was up to 44kW (60bhp), but a long stroke kept maximum rpm down to just 3000 rpm.

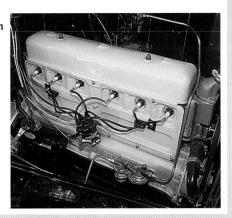

Handling

Both cars have solid axle suspensions and ride on tall 45cm (18in) wheels and tires. Therefore, both behave in a similar way, tending to roll under heavier throttle openings. The Chevy is, arguably, slightly better.

Performance

With 44kW (60bhp) from its sidevalve six, the Chevy is incredibly slow by modern standards but offered enough go to satisfy most folks in 1932. The Ford, in view of its flathead V8 engine, has a distinct advantage here. It has more mid-range punch and has a higher top speed, although few drivers will attempt to reach it.

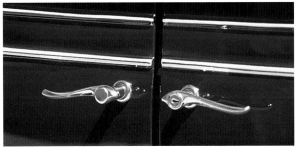

Ford MODEL 18

Inside Story

With the company still firmly under Henry's control in 1932, Fords were still built as inexpensively as possible. The Model 18 was firmly based on its Model A predecessor, with a separate ladder-type steel chassis that was essentially unchanged, apart from a slightly longer wheelbase. The suspension is primitive but, by 1930s standards, still effective. At the front is a solid beam axle, sprung by a transverse leaf spring with lever arm shocks. The live rear axle is also sprung by a transverse leaf. Four wheel brakes are fitted, but these are mechanically, instead of hydraulically, activated.

POWER PACK

Ford's biggest news for 1932 was the arrival of its new V8 in March. Created under the guidance of Henry himself, the V8 went from concept to market as soon as possible. Although an excellent design, the cast-iron valve-in-block engine was not given sufficient durability testing and reliability problems – mainly piston and bearing failure – were common initially. Nevertheless, with 48kW (65bhp), it succeeded in turning Fords into real performers.

Accommodation

Interior styling is similar in both cars, with bench seats, huge steering wheels and flat windows all around. The Confederate is more comfortable and feels slightly more upmarket. It also has a smoother shifting transmission, making it slightly easier to drive than the Ford over greater distances.

Ride

An appropriate description for the ride quality of these cars is rock hard, but on rough surfaces this does not change noticeably – a reminder of 1930s road conditions.

▇▇ Ford MUSTANG MACH 1

It is impossible to imagine a world where Camaro and Mustang are not rivals. In the late 1960s, Chevrolet built the huge-engined SS396TM, but how did it match up against the Mustang Mach 1 with even more engine capacity?

Affordable, compact, and performance-orientated, the Mustang was the sales phenomenon that took America by storm and single-handedly created a new class of automobile – the pony car. Keen to get in on the action, other manufacturers copied the formula to come up with their own pony cars to rival the Mustang, and the Chevrolet Camaro is its most direct and fiercest competitor.

It might have looked like an entirely new car on the outside, but underneath the Mustang relied on a chassis and underpinnings from lesser cars in the Ford canon to keep costs down, although a fantastic options list pushed the price up and meant cars could be tailored to suit an owner's individual requirements.

With more power than traction, both cars will happily spin their wheels when trying to pull away in hurry, but the Mustang will do so less than the Camaro, making it the faster car away from the line.

With massive V8 engines up front, both cars feel nose heavy, but the Mustang has the edge on handling and greater feel from its heavier steering, informing the driver of what is happening and giving a better sense of control. Others may come close, but the legendary Mustang is still the king of all muscle cars.

FORD MUSTANG MACH 1

Engine Capacity	7015cc (428cu in)
Weight	1633kg (3601lb)
Power	250kW (335bhp)
Torque	597.9Nm (441lb-ft) @ 3400 rpm
Price	$3139

Acceleration:

0–30mph (48km/h)	2.2 sec.
0–60mph (96km/h)	5.7 sec.
0–100mph (160km/h)	14.4 sec.
Standing ¼ mile (400m)	14.3 sec.
Maximum Speed	190km/h (118mph)

Chevrolet CAMARO SS396TM

CHEVROLET CAMARO SS396TM

Engine Capacity	6490cc (396cu in)
Weight	1583kg (3491lb)
Power	279kW (375bhp)
Torque	562.7Nm (415lb-ft) @ 3600 rpm
Price	$4294
Acceleration:	
0–30mph (48km/h)	2.6 sec.
0–60mph (96km/h)	6.8 sec.
0–100mph (160km/h)	15.6 sec.
Standing 1/4 mile (400m)	14.8 sec.
Maximum Speed	203km/h (126mph)

In the world of the '60s muscle car, power was everything. and the Camaro came with more ponies under its hood than its fiercest competitor, the Mustang. So, while it may not be as quick away from the lights as its rival, the Camaro produces more power and has the higher top speed.

In its day, the Camaro was one of the best handling American sports cars available, and still hangs in there when the Mustang has reached the limits of its grip. Added to which, the Camaro has the softer suspension, so offers a smoother ride for its passengers under more civilized driving conditions. Nor does it roll or lean as fiercely as the Mustang.

The Mustang may have offered the longer options list, but the standard Camaro is the more comfortable car. Inside the cabin it has wider, more comfortable seats than the Ford and more generous amounts of room, with space for two in the back to make it more family friendly than the fastback pony.

The Camaro was Chevrolet's flagship car, but its top model with all the performance options included only cost $1000 more than the standard spec Mustang – a difference that was soon ironed out when the Ford customer began adding equipment – making the Camaro a muscle-car bargain.

Ford MUSTANG MACH 1

Inside Story

Ford tried to match the chassis to the big engine. The basic suspension design is little changed from the earlier Mustangs, but the front coil springs and rear leaf springs are both stiffer, the shocks have been uprated to match, and the anti-roll bar is thicker. In addition, the tire width has been increased to 15cm (6in). The front-heavy weight distribution means that power steering is virtually a necessity, as are the power brakes.

P O W E R   P A C K

The cast-iron Cobra Jet pushrod V8 has more than sheer size going for it. Back in the days when fuel was good quality, it could run a high 10.6:1 compression ratio and its cylinder head design was excellent, allowing it to breathe easily and rev high. Fed by a four-barrel Holley carb, it produces its maximum 246kW (335bhp) – which may be a conservative estimate – at 5200 rpm.

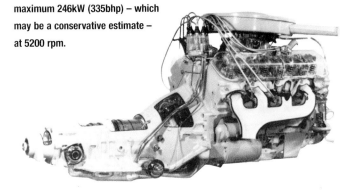

Performance

The Mustang has greater torque and can apply its power far better than the Camaro. The Ford has a one-second advantage in reaching 96km/h (60mph) and is even further ahead by 160km/h (100mph). It may not be able to match the SS396's top speed, but in terms of acceleration, the Mustang wins.

Braking

Both cars have power disks at the front and drums at the rear, but the Mustang's are larger due to their greater weight. Both systems have good feel, but both fade under heavy and repeated use, which isn't uncommon for cars of this era. The diameters of both cars are small, compared to the brake systems on today's cars. In 1969, neither Chevrolet nor Mustang put as much technology in their cars.

Chevrolet CAMARO SS396TM

Inside Story

Standard Camaro suspension is stiffened to cope with the extra power of the big 6489cc (396cu in) engine. The front anti-roll bar diameter is larger to help combat understeer. The live rear axle, with its simple semi-elliptic leaf spring, has staggered shock absorbers to help deal with axle tramp. Make no mistake, though, this car was built for straight-line acceleration. It quickly became a muscle car icon of the 1960s and it's no wonder why it was chosen to pace the 1969 Indy 500.

POWER PACK

Big and oversquare (10 x 9.5cm/4 x 3.76in), this V8 may be old Detroit iron, but with its solid valve lifters, 11.0:1 compression ratio and four-barrel Holley, it will rev to 6300 rpm and produces a staggering amount of power (276kW/375bhp). It is a sportier engine than the Mustang's, and despite giving away 524cc (32cu in), it still produces more power. The 291/275kW (396/375bhp) engine is the highest-powered engine available in regular production Camaros.

Road holding

They have the same size tires and similar suspension designs, producing a very close contest. The Mustang's tires seem to start screeching earlier and it reaches its ultimate limits of grip slightly sooner, putting the Camaro ahead in terms of holding the road.

Accommodation

The Mustang Mach 1 has new seats with integral headrests, which hold the driver in place well but are a bit thin. The Camaro's seats are comfortable and its steering wheel is elegant. There is room for four people to relax in comfort – an area in which the fastback 2+2 Mustang loses out.

Ferrari 365 GT/4

Four-seater supercars are as rare as they are fast. Ferrari, the masters of the grand tourer, faced stiff competition in the 1970s when Lamborghini launched the Espada. But which one has the bragging rights as being the best in its class?

Whether you prefer the sight of a prancing horse or raging bull on your hood is a matter of personal choice. But whichever you settle on, you'll have room for all the family to enjoy it in the 365 GTC/4 – even though the idea of a four-seat "practical" Ferrari was anathema to die-hard enthusiasts.

If the Espada looks a bit too like an old Volkswagen Passat for you, at least the Ferrari looks like a proper Ferrari, with its curvaceous bodywork and traditionally exotic appearance. It drives like a proper sports car should too, so there's

absolutely no sign of a compromised chassis design when driven flat-out into corners. Agile and responsive as all good Ferraris should be, the 365 has more involving steering than the Lambo and just feels the more exciting car to drive on the road, even if the figures on paper don't quite match up to the reality.

Neither machine is as popular as the rest of its two-seater stablemates, but when it comes down to it, the more flamboyant Ferrari always was, and always will be, the more desirable and expensive one to own.

FERRARI 365 GT/4

Engine Capacity	4390cc (269 ci)
Weight	1734kg (3825lb)
Power	240kW (320bhp)
Torque	431Nm (318lb-ft) @ 4000 rpm
Price	$27,500
Acceleration:	
0–30mph (48km/h)	2.8 sec.
0–60mph (96km/h)	7.3 sec.
0–100mph (160km/h)	9.3 sec.
Standing ¼ mile (400m)	15.2 sec.
Maximum Speed	245km/h (152mph)

Lamborghini ESPADA

LAMBORGHINI ESPADA

Engine Capacity	3929cc (240 ci)
Weight	1666kg (3675lb)
Power	290kW (390bhp)
Torque	433Nm (320lb-ft) @ 5000 rpm
Price	$21,000
Acceleration:	
0–30mph (48km/h)	2.7 sec.
0–60mph (96km/h)	6.5 sec.
0–100mph (160km/h)	7.9 sec.
Standing ¼ mile (400m)	16.1 sec.
Maximum Speed	254km/h (158mph)

Always fierce rivals, if Ferrari wanted to build a four-seat supercar, then Lamborghini had to do the same, and as usual, they believed they'd do a better job.

Amazingly, for a manufacturer of some of the world's most exotic and potent supercars, its four-seat grand tourer became the most successful Lamborghini of all time. With an extra row of seats shoved in the back, there's no room for a mid-mounted engine, so the V12s in both the Ferrari and Lamborghini are up front. Each unit is capable of propelling these cars to more than 240km/h (150mph), although the Espada will get there quicker and still keep going when the Ferrari runs out of steam at 244km/h (152mph).

The Espada is slightly larger, and has more traction and grip. Its composed chassis copes admirably with twists and turns, and body roll is less pronounced. With four seats and a lift-up rear hatch, the Espada is as practical a Lamborghini as they come. It's just a pity that it looks so similar to its creator Giorgetto Giugiaro's subsequent design, the Volkswagen Passat, from certain angles.

Ferrari 365 GT/4

Inside Story

Ferrari has a strong history of four-seater cars. The 365 GTC/4 is a direct development of the pure-bred Daytona sports coupe and shares its tubular chassis. The all-independent suspension including Koni self-leveling rear shock absorbers and four-wheel disk brakes is also carried over. Unlike the 365 GTB/4 Daytona, however, the GTC employs a conventional transmission in place of the rear-mounted five-speed transaxle.

POWER PACK

The 365 GTC/4's engine can be traced back to 1947 when Gioacchino Colombo designed the company's first V12. By 1971, it had been expanded to 4.4l and developed between 235 and 250kW (320 and 340bhp). It has four camshafts (two per bank of cylinders), an aluminum block and heads and six Weber 38 DCOE twin-barrel carburetors. This engine survived in the later 365 GT/4 and 400, the latter with a stroked 4.8-l version.

Accommodation

The Ferrari emerges as the winner here because there is space for tall passengers in the back with reasonable legroom, as well as a generous trunk. While the Espada offers comfortable seating in the rear, there isn't nearly as much available headroom as there is in the Ferrari.

Handling

In terms of poise and response, the 365 GTC/4 is superior. The Espada handles competently, but there is more of a sense of unwanted drama than in the Ferrari.

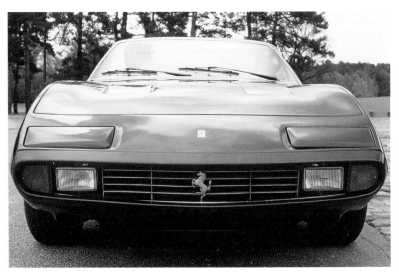

Lamborghini ESPADA

Inside Story

The Espada's 264cm (104.3in) wheelbase is 10cm (4in) longer than other Lamborghinis and it has a pressed-steel chassis. The front-mounted engine, steering and four-wheel disk brakes are shared with the earlier 400 GT. The suspension is an effective mix of unequal-length A-arms and coil springs at each end with two anti-roll bars. Initially, a five-speed manual transmission was the only choice, but the market demanded an automatic, so Lamborghini obliged.

POWER PACK

The V12 quad-cam engine in the Espada was a jewel to rival any Ferrari engine. Its 4.0l (244cu in) displacement may be relatively small for a V12, but it does not lack power. In its original guise, it developed 239kW (325bhp), but that rose to 257kW (350bhp) in the Series II version and to 286kW (390bhp) at 7500 rpm in the Series III. Its block and heads are made of aluminum and there are six Weber twin-barrel carburetors.

Performance

Both cars are powered by V12 engines, so any difference in performance comes down to weight and gearing. The Espada is heavier and, as it makes more horsepower on paper, it is faster to 96km/h (60mph) than the Ferrari. At higher rpm though, the Lamborghini really comes into its own.

Ride

Ride is important when carrying four passengers. Although the suspension on the two cars are designed for sharp cornering, neither is uncomfortable. However, the Ferrari's self-leveling suspension provides the same level of ride quality regardless of the load. Its ride is great for a sports car. In comparison, when full, the Lamborghini stiffens and ride suffers.

Ferrari 330

In the early 1960s, Ferraris were regarded as the best road/race cars in the world. Then along came the Ford GT40, which won a record four times at Le Mans. So how does Henry's marvel stack up against the illustrious competition?

As phenomenal as the GT40 is on the race track, Ferrari doesn't have a reputation for greatness for nothing. Statistically speaking, the 330 is only fractionally behind the Ford in every respect – just 0.4 of a second slower in the race to 160km/h (100mph), which it will accomplish in 15.8 seconds flat – so it's certainly no slouch. But the Ferrari has another card up its sleeve. It's a fantastic car for the road as well as the track, so you don't need to be insane, an expert driver, or have a massive ego to use it there.

In truth, as awesome as the GT40 is, it is just a little too full on. It's simply too dedicated to speed, whereas the 330

makes more concessions to passenger comfort and practicality, which is not something you hear too often in connection with a Ferrari. It's easier to climb into, see out of, and use at sensible speeds, yet is still regarded as one the finest-handling cars ever made.

Not as aerodynamic as the more race-orientated Ford, the 330 is arguably the more attractive of the two. It's simply stunning from any angle, so for show the Ferrari wins, but for track use alone, it would probably be the GT40, but only just.

FERRARI 330

Engine Capacity	3967cc (242cu in)
Weight	984kg (2170lb)
Power	298kW (400bhp)
Torque	447.4Nm (330lb-ft) @ 5500 rpm
Price	$21,000
Acceleration:	
0–30mph (48km/h)	2.1 sec.
0–60mph (96km/h)	5.6 sec.
0–100mph (160km/h)	15.8 sec.
Standing ¼ mile (400m)	13.5 sec.
Maximum Speed	290km/h (180mph)

Ford GT40

FORD GT40

Engine Capacity	4736cc (289cu in)
Weight	832kg (1835lb)
Power	276kW (370bhp)
Torque	433.9Nm (320lb-ft) @ 6000 rpm
Price	$18,000
Acceleration:	
0–30mph (48km/h)	2.0 sec.
0–60mph (96km/h)	5.5 sec.
0–100mph (160km/h)	15.4 sec.
Standing ¼ mile (400m)	13.1 sec.
Maximum Speed	298km/h (185mph)

Ford versus a Ferrari? Ordinarily it would be no contest, but then the GT40 is no ordinary blue oval. This is the legendary racing car that won the grueling Le Mans 24 Hours a record number of times and beat some of the greatest names in racing along the way. If Ferrari wasn't scarlet before the GT40 burst onto the scene, it certainly was after.

But is it really so good? Just take a look at it. The Ferrari is undeniably beautiful, stunning even, but few cars look more like they've just driven straight off a race track – or stand as low – as the GT40. Its low center of gravity is one of its keys to success, endowing it with truly superb cornering and amazing aerodynamics. Few cars, not even the 330, will keep up with it as it lunges to an eventual top speed of 298km/h (185mph).

However, its height is also the GT40's major drawback. Standing just 101cm (40in) tall – hence its name – the Ford isn't as usable or practical as the Ferrari. Tall people will struggle to fit inside, visibility is poor, and they might not be able to close the door over their heads. Sitting at the same height as most truck wheels is horribly disconcerting and, to add to that, you'll be expected to pay through the nose for the privilege.

Ferrari 330

Inside Story

The success of the 250 GTO left Ferrari engineers pondering how a more aerodynamic version might fare at Le Mans. So the 330 LMB was born. It uses a long-wheelbase version of the GTO chassis with Lusso-style bodywork. The suspension follows familiar practice, with a coil-and-wishbone independent front end and a well located live axle on semi-elliptic leaf springs and co-axial shocks. Dunlop disk brakes provide awesome stopping power.

POWER PACK

In Ferrari's numbering system, 330 indicates the individual cylinder displacement. Hence, the Tipo 163 V12 twin overhead camshaft engine in the 330 LMB measures 4.0l, as had been used in the last GTOs. The compression ratio is 9.0:1 (compared with 8.7:1 in the GTO), which helps the engine to develop 294kW (400bhp) at 7500 rpm. No fewer than six Weber 42DCN downdraft carburetors nestle neatly under the long hood.

Accommodation

The Ferrari wins hands down here because of its front-engined layout and its alter ego as a road car. In contrast, the GT40 is a pure racer with a tight cockpit. Getting in over the huge sills is far from easy.

Performance

Both cars have engines with near-equal amounts of power. The big difference is in the cars' weight. Ferrari claims 984kg (2170lb) for the 330, whereas the GT40 tips the scales at just 832kg (1835lb). That gives the Ford a distinct edge in acceleration. Both cars are superbly aerodynamic, but again, the Ford has a smaller frontal area because it's so low to the ground.

Inside Story

The story goes that the GT40 was conceived to beat Ferrari at Le Mans after Ford's attempt to buy the legendary Italian company failed. The design, by Eric Broadley and John Wyer, features a semi-monocoque chassis fitted with glass-fibre body panels made in the US and delivered to a factory in Slough, UK. At the front end are dual control arms with coil springs, and at the rear there are dual trailing arms, transverse links, lower control arms, and coils. Anti-roll bars are fitted at both ends.

P O W E R   P A C K

The first 1964 GT40 had a 256cu in, all-alloy, Ford V8 engine, but most were fitted with the cast-iron block, 4736cc (289cu in) motor. This was fitted with four Weber twin-barrel carburetors and originally rated at 272kW (370bhp) at 6700 rpm. Roadgoing GT40s have lower-compression engines. A handful of Mark II, J-type and Mark IV models use the 7000cc (427cu in) Ford V8, which boasts between 356 and 368kW (485 and 500bhp) at 6200 or 5000 rpm.

Handling

The 330 LMB is a beautifully balanced racer and has superb axle location. Nevertheless, the limitations of a leaf-sprung rear axle eventually become evident at the limit. The GT40 also offers remarkable handling balance, but it adds an agility that the Ferrari simply cannot match.

Road holding

Because of its height, the GT40 has an ultra-low center of gravity and therefore boasts amazing amounts of grip. It can be confidently cornered at very high speeds. The Ferrari has great chassis balance, but its tires seem to run out of grip well before those of the GT40.

Ford MUSTANG GT

Camaro versus Mustang battles have been raging since the 1960s and both cars are still going strong in the 1990s. The question still remains, however. How do they fare against each other in the real world?

Their looks may have changed out of all recognition, but the thinking behind and rivalry between the Mustang and Camaro has never changed. However, the Mustang now sports the more angular and aggressive styling, so is arguably the more attractive machine, in a conventional sense, while the sleek, almost bland-looking Camaro now looks more Japanese than American.

It gets worse for the Camaro when you look inside its cabin. Its ergonomics and driving position are not a patch on the Mustang's and being $2500 cheaper is no excuse. On a longer journey you'll find yourself wishing you'd dug a little deeper and stumped up the $27,870 for the comfier and better thought-out Mustang.

A wide track and big ZR-series tires do a surprisingly good job of keeping the Ford's old Fox platform on the straight and narrow and, considering it was originally conceived way back in 1978, the Mustang's chassis provides an excellent ride which is noticeably smoother over rougher surfaces than the Camaro.

Neither machine is vastly superior to the other in any one respect, but when all is said and done, the road-hugging, more attractive and sporty Mustang is the one most of us would prefer to have sitting in our garage. Even after all these years, it's still a keenly priced sports car for the masses.

FORD MUSTANG

Engine Capacity	5.7l (348cu in)
Weight	1470kg (3242lb)
Power	191kW (260bhp)
Torque	597.9Nm (441lb-ft) @ 3400 rpm
Price	$27,875
Acceleration:	
0–30mph (48km/h)	2.1 sec.
0–60mph (96km/h)	5.5 sec.
0–100mph (160km/h)	14.5 sec.
Standing ¼ mile (400m)	14.1 sec.
Maximum Speed	240km/h (150mph)

Chevrolet CAMARO Z28

CHEVROLET CAMARO Z28

Engine Capacity	4.6l (281cu in)
Weight	1623kg (3578lb)
Power	224kW (305bhp)
Torque	562.7Nm (415lb-ft) @ 3600 rpm
Price	$25,361
Acceleration:	
0–30mph (48km/h)	2.0 sec.
0–60mph (96km/h)	5.2 sec.
0–100mph (160km/h)	14.3 sec.
Standing ¼ mile (400m)	13.7 sec.
Maximum Speed	260km/h (160mph)

What exactly happened to the Camaro? In this form it looks so bland and characterless it's almost nondescript compared to its ancestors. The long process of evolution rounded and smoothed its once aggressive looks and love it or loathe it, you have to admit it now boasts an aerodynamic sleekness the angular Mustang lacks.

It might not seem as aggressive as the Mustang, but the Camaro has the edge when it comes to power and acceleration. A full 16km/h (10mph) faster when traveling flat-out, the Z28 is also quicker across the board and will only run out of steam when it gets to 260km/h (160mph), so it's fast by any standards.

Power is nothing without handling, and the Camaro delights in this field too. Live axles are hardly the last word in technology, but jab the throttle and you can invoke plenty of useable oversteer, so it feels like a proper muscle car from behind the wheel.

Even fully loaded with every option available, the Z28 weighs in at a wallet-friendly $26,000. With so much performance per dollar, the Camaro offers a huge amount of bang for your bucks, and is still an undoubted performance-car bargain.

Ford MUSTANG GT

Inside Story

The 1999 Mustang is the sole surviving example of a Fox platform Ford, which began way back in 1978 with the Fairmont. When redesigned for the 1994 model year, the Mustang got a much stiffer unibody with extra bracing for convertibles. The platform, with modified MacPherson struts up front and a coil-sprung live rear axle received a few improvements for 1999, namely a wider rear track and greater suspension travel, plus revised shocks and anti-roll bars to improve handling.

POWER PACK

In 1998, Mustang GTs got a new engine in the form of the 4.6-liter overhead-cam "modular" V8. Rated at 158kW (215bhp), it gave the Mustang GT reasonable performance, but it was no match for the Z28. Thanks to intake modifications in 1998, power was bumped up to 165kW (225bhp). In 1999, power jumped to a formidable 191kW (260bhp) and torque to 409Nm (302lb-ft). This is mainly because of higher lift, longer-duration cams, bigger valves and a revised intake system.

Accommodation

The Camaro's front buckets do a great job of supporting the driver and front passenger, but the ergonomics and driving position leave a lot to be desired, especially over longer distances. The Mustang, by comparison, offers better outward visibility, easier-to-use controls and greater comfort on long journeys.

Ride

Razor-sharp handling translates into a billboard-like ride for the Z28. The Mustang GT, with retuned shocks for 1999, feels noticeably smoother and more compliant on bumpy roads.

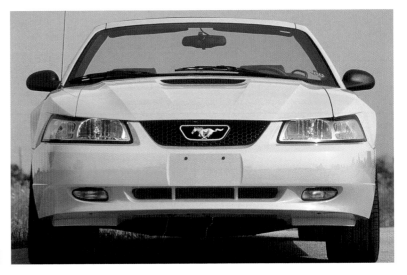

Chevrolet CAMARO Z28

Inside Story

With a stiffer chassis, new front suspension design and an all-new body with many panels made from dent-resistant plastic composite, the Camaro was heavily re-engineered for the 1993 model year. Like previous generations, however, the car is still a rear-drive, live-axle machine, with a torque arm and Panhard rod to help control lateral movement. Anti-lock, four-wheel disk brakes are standard on Z28s, as are dual exhausts and dual catalytic convertors.

POWER PACK

From 1993 until 1997, the Z28's heart was the 5735cc (350cu in) LT1, with aluminum heads. Cranking out 202kW (275bhp) (209kW/285 from 1996), it made the Z28 a formidable performer. For 1998, the LT1 was replaced by a brand new small-block V8, the 5735cc (350cu in) all-aluminum LS1. While the displacement stays the same, the rest of the engine is all new. Rated at 224kW (305bhp) and 454Nm (335lb-ft), it makes the Z28 a sub-6-second 0–96km/h (0–60mph) machine.

Performance

With an increase in power and torque output, the Mustang GT feels a lot stronger, especially midway through the rpm range where it really comes into its own. Even so, the Camaro Z28 still has the edge and is noticeably quicker at all engine speeds.

Road holding

On the track, the Z28 feels a bit more eager and demonstrates marginally better poise. In the real world, however, the difference is less noticeable. Both cars, with their meaty Z-rated rubber, hold the line well, though live axles mean that power on oversteer is still easily invoked.

⊞ Triumph TR6

It's a battle between the last of the traditional old-fashioned British sports cars and the first of a new breed of powerful modern performance coupes – one good enough to become the world's best sports car. Does the Triumph stand a chance?

In its day the TR6 was Triumph's best-selling sports car. Always a strong seller on both sides of the Atlantic, the majority of the 94,000 or so built found homes in America. The TR6 offered all the appeal of a traditional British roadster, but was faster and more entertaining than many of its would-be rivals. Its combination of power and typical Triumph virtues goes a long way to explaining why it's still so popular today and is still widely regarded by many as the last of the true TRs.

The TR6 is arguably the more macho-looking machine of the pair and while it might be noisier and less refined than the Datsun, this is one of its more appealing traits. It's fun and involving to power through twists and curves that the 240Z negotiates with a lesser sense of occasion or fuss.

The Triumph also feels more like a sports car in the traditional sense, with a folding roof, wooden fascia and lots of typical British craftsmanship on display. The Datsun, by contrast, has a fixed metal roof and a less inspiring interior with fewer gauges and plenty of sombre black plastic on display.

It might be the more demanding machine to live with, but when did practicality matter when choosing a sports car?

TRIUMPH TR6

Engine Capacity	2498cc (152cu in)
Weight	1123kg (2476lb)
Power	112kW (150bhp)
Torque	222.4Nm (164lb-ft) @ 3000 rpm
Price	$3375
Acceleration:	
0–60mph (96km/h)	8.4 sec.
0–80mph (128km/h)	15.3 sec.
0–100mph (160km/h)	29.0 sec.
Standing ¼ mile (400m)	16.3 sec.
Maximum Speed	191km/h (119mph)

Datsun 240Z

DATSUN 240Z

Engine Capacity	2393cc (146cu in)
Weight	1089kg (2401lb)
Power	113kW (151bhp)
Torque	197.9Nm (146lb-ft) @ 4400 rpm
Price	$3526
Acceleration:	
0–60mph (96km/h)	8.2 sec.
0–80mph (128km/h)	14.4 sec.
0–100mph (160km/h)	23.9 sec.
Standing ¼ mile (400m)	16.2 sec.
Maximum Speed	201km/h (125mph)

With a cleverly thought-out display of "anything you can do we can do better", Japan gave birth to the Datsun 240Z. There had been other sports cars from Japan but the 240Z was the first to take on and break the European stranglehold on the affordable sports car market. It was phenomenally successful because it was fast, cheaper than the competition, and more reliable.

The 240Z might be the low-cost, more reliable option but that doesn't make it any less exciting. You get your kicks in a different way in the Datsun, because it's the smoother, more

usable, and refined of the pair. While the Triumph feels like a big, heavy, handful, the Datsun can be used by anyone, for anything, whether it is carving up challenging, twisty roads or simply fetching your weekly shopping.

The handling and performance from either machine will put a smile on your face, but the Datsun has the more advanced suspension, which means there is virtually no body roll even at speed. It's also more predictable and returns more feel through the steering wheel. Purists may sneer about the Datsun's Japanese roots, but as a fun classic coupe you can use everyday, it's certainly the smarter choice.

Triumph TR6

Inside Story

A strong and heavy separate chassis was retained for the TR6, with four hefty longitudinal rails. Double wishbone suspension is used at the front with coil springs, telescopic shocks and anti-roll bar. At the rear is an independent set-up: semi-trailing arms, coil springs and lever-arm shocks. Although the transmission is only a four-speed, it has a superb overdrive which operates on 2nd, 3rd and 4th gears, effectively giving seven forward speeds.

P O W E R   P A C K

The enduring appeal of the TR6 is due to the long-stroke straight-six engine. It may seem fairly low tech in having a single camshaft and cast-iron block with the exhaust and intake on the same side, but with its high (9.5:1) compression ratio and Lucas fuel injection it pumps out a very smooth 110kW (150bhp) in European trim. US specification TR6s produce 76kW (104bhp) due to the addition of emissions equipment and small twin Stromberg carburetors.

Handling

On a dry, smooth road, the ultra-stiff TR6 comes into its own. Its consistent understeer is reassuring and there are no surprises. In the wet it is easily thrown off line by bumps and is hard to correct. The Z is better all around, its superior suspension giving progressive, yet safe, handling.

Accommodation

The seats in neither are perfect, nor is the driving position. The TR's steering wheel feels too close, while short drivers feel buried in the Z. As befitting a British car, the TR has a wooden dashboard and lots of gauges. In contrast, the Z has deep set gauges and plastic everywhere. Here it is up to individual choice.

Datsun 240Z

Inside Story

Datsun opted for a modern unitary construction monocoque with the 240Z, which was also one of the first sports cars to use MacPherson struts as both the front and rear suspension (a feature employed on many modern cars). Like the Triumph, it has rack-and-pinion steering, but in place of a heavy overdrive transmission it has a five-speed manual. A short wheelbase combined with a wide track results in fine handling. Like the TR, it has front discs and rear drum brakes.

P O W E R   P A C K

The Z has an iron-block, alloy-head straight-six engine, but it is a short-stroke design 8 x 7.5cm (3.27 x 3in) with an overhead camshaft and is thus higher revving than the TR unit. It has two valves per cylinder and a 9.0:1 compression ratio with fuel fed in by twin Japanese Hitachi carburetors. Early US specification 240Z sixes were rated at 151bhp (111kW) and 197Nm (146lb-ft) of torque, which is more than a match for the TR6 in the US.

Performance

The TR and Datsun Z are extremely close when it comes to performance. There is absolutely nothing between them in terms of outright acceleration up to 96km/h (60mph) and through the standing ¼-mile (400m). It is only at higher speeds that the Datsun gains the advantage due to its superior aerodynamics.

Ride

Although both cars employ independent suspension, the Z with its MacPherson struts and superior geometry gives a smoother ride than the TR, which can be jarring on rough roads.

Ford CUSTOM 300

If you ask most people today which is the definitive 1950s car, most will say a 1957 Chevy, but arch-rival Ford actually sold more cars that year. In top form, both are strong runners, but how do they measure up against each other?

Possibly not the most agile 1950s throwback money can buy, the Custom 300 has the look nonetheless, even if it didn't have the build quality or caring owners to ensure very many survive today.

Lower, longer, and wider than previous Fords, the Custom 300 looks remarkably similar to the Chevy, but it's a different story underneath its heavily finned metal skin. Its chassis and suspension are more advanced than the Bel Air's dual A-arms and coil springs up front, but there's not a great deal to choose between them when it comes to handling, as both were softly sprung to deal with poor road conditions and shod in tall, skinny crossply tyres. The upshot of this is that neither corners well, but both are comfortable long-distance cruisers.

More torque means more grunt and lowdown performance, and that's exactly what the Ford has over the Chevy. Its gruffer, less refined V8 makes it feel the more rapid machine and supercharged versions even more so – if you can find one that is.

The more capable driver's machine, the only area that lets the Ford down is its inferior build quality when compared to the Bel Air. Ultimately, it is always quality that counts, so the Chevrolet wins the battle.

FORD CUSTOM 300

Engine Capacity	5260cc (321cu in)
Weight	1226kg (3284lb)
Power	224kW (300bhp)
Torque	455.6Nm (336lb-ft) @ 3400 rpm
Price	$2205
Acceleration:	
0–30mph (48km/h)	2.3 sec.
0–60mph (96km/h)	7.5 sec.
0–100mph (160km/h)	17.4 sec.
Standing ¼ mile (400m)	15.9 sec.
Maximum Speed	201km/h (125mph)

Chevrolet BEL AIR

CHEVROLET BEL AIR

Engine Capacity	4637cc (283cu in)
Weight	1024kg (3228lb)
Power	211kW (283bhp)
Torque	393.2Nm (290lb-ft) @ 4400 rpm
Price	$2338

Acceleration:

0–30mph (48km/h)	2.7 sec.
0–60mph (96km/h)	7.5 sec.
0–100mph (160km/h)	17.8 sec.
Standing 1/4 mile (400m)	16.2 sec.
Maximum Speed	201km/h (125mph)

Fins were most definitely "in" when these rock 'n' roll classics rolled off their production lines back in 1957 and they still have a lure and appeal that makes them as popular now as they ever have been.

There's just something about a heavily chromed, massively finned, and vibrantly painted Chevy that people love, and a 50s Bel Air is to many minds the ultimate American-built classic. This one-time mainstream sedan is now a major collector's piece. Incredibly fast in its day, it still impresses now.

Despite its smaller-capacity motor, the Chevy will match the Ford for top-speed but take fractionally more time to reach it. In fuel-injected form it produces a not unimpressive 211kW (283bhp). It feels smoother, if less powerful than the Ford.

The Bel Air's underpinnings were designed before the Ford's and show their age more. As a result, the Chevy doesn't feel as sure-footed or well planted as its rival. Perhaps the ultimate expression of Detroit iron, the '57 Bel Air might not be as great a mover or shaker as the Custom 300, but it's better built, costs more, and is the more collectable now.

Ford CUSTOM 300

Inside Story

Ford offered a completely new design for 1957, which was lower, longer and wider than its predecessor. Under the skin, it differs little from the previous model. It has a separate, perimeter-type steel chassis and an independent front suspension with dual A-arms and coil springs. At the rear is a live axle on semi-elliptic leaf springs. Customs rode a 294cm (116in) wheelbase (Fairlanes rode 300cm/118in). Four-wheel drum brakes were standard on all 1957 Fords.

P O W E R   P A C K

By 1957, an inline six was standard in the Ford lineup, though an assortment of Y-block V8s were available. The largest was the 5113cc (312cu in) Thunderbird special engine, which, with a four-barrel Holley carburetor, was rated at 180kW (245bhp). A very small number of regular Fords got a supercharged version. This car has a McCulloch/Paxton centrifugal supercharger, a more aggressive camshaft, different intake manifold and cylinder heads.

Accommodation

Front and rear legroom in both cars is good and the bench seats are fairly comfortable, so preferences on the cabin ambience come down to a question of personal taste. The Chevy has a more inspiring dashboard and is better equipped than the austere Ford.

Handling

Skinny, biasply tires, soft springs and very light steering translate into precarious handling, especially at higher speeds. The Ford, with more weight up front, understeers to a greater degree through the turns.

Chevrolet BEL AIR

Inside Story

Chevrolet's model lineup had been all new for 1955, and the 1957 version was essentially a cosmetic update. Like the Ford, it employs body-on-the-frame construction, with a separate steel chassis. Suspension is also in the traditional '50s Detroit design: dual A-arms and coil springs at the front, plus a live axle and semi-elliptic leaf springs at the rear. Transmission choices included a three- or four-speed manual and Powerglide two-speed automatic. Drum brakes are fitted front and rear.

POWER PACK

One of the greatest engines of all time, the classic small-block Chevy V8 began life in 1955 as a 4342cc (265cu in) unit. This five main-bearing, cast-iron V8 was bored to 283 cubes for 1957 and was available in five different states of tune. Top of the line was the fuelie motor. It received this nickname because it shunned carburetors in preference to Rochester mechanical fuel injection. Packing an advertised 208kW (283bhp), it was powerful but required frequent tuning.

Performance

Packing 208kW (283bhp) from its fuel-injected small-block, this Chevrolet is smooth and torquey, its only drawback being the two-speed Powerglide. The Ford has the greater advantage. With its 220kW (300bhp) and greater torque, Henry's car is quicker.

Ride

Fairly soft springs, designed to cope with poor road surfaces, mean each car is comfortable for freeway cruising, but ultimately, the Chevy does a better job at reducing vibration.

Chevrolet CAMARO Z-28

Both the muscle car wars and Trans-Am racing reached new heights in 1970. The Camaro Z-28 and 'Cuda AAR were among the baddest of the homologation specials, but when the dust settles, how do they really measure up?

While the Barracuda was intended to be a factory street-rod, the special edition Z28 was built to look like a full-on racecar. Not only that, but the second generation Camaro was more shark-like and macho than ever before – a muscle car on steroids, no less.

The Camaro's reworked styling breathed new life into the model at a time when many manufacturers were predicting the imminent demise of the pony car. In fact, it proved so popular the Camaro soldiered on in this form for 12 years. There were plenty of changes under the skin, including an all-new V8 and a highly impressive terminal velocity of 206km/h (128mph), so it talks the talk and walks the walk. Even if you prefer the Barracuda's tail-in-the-air stance, there's little chance you'll prefer the way it handles. Its huge rear tires and uneven ride height make it feel more unbalanced than the Camaro at speed, and more nose-heavy as it dives into corners.

Both are muscular 2+2s, with mean-sized interiors. However, the Camaro's bucket seats are more supportive and comfortable in both the front and the back, and if you had to pick one for regular use, it would have to be the Z-28.

CHEVROLET CAMARO Z-28

Engine Capacity	5735cc (350cu in)
Weight	1485kg (3275lb)
Power	268kW (360bhp)
Torque	467.8Nm (345lb-ft) @ 3400 rpm
Price	$3410
Acceleration:	
0–30mph (48km/h)	2.1 sec.
0–60mph (96km/h)	6.1 sec.
0–100mph (160km/h)	14.8 sec.
Standing ¼ mile (400m)	14.4 sec.
Maximum Speed	206km/h (128mph)

Plymouth CUDA AAR

PLYMOUTH CUDA AAR

Engine Capacity	5570cc (340cu in)
Weight	1549kg (3415lb)
Power	253kW (340bhp)
Torque	515.2Nm (380lb-ft) @ 4000 rpm
Price	$3490
Acceleration:	
0–30mph (48km/h)	2.0 sec.
0–60mph (96km/h)	5.8 sec.
0–100mph (160km/h)	14.7 sec.
Standing ¼ mile (400m)	14.4 sec.
Maximum speed	201km/h (125mph)

It's widely acknowledged that the Ford Mustang kick-started the pony-car revolution, but did you know the Plymouth Barracuda actually got there first? Unfortunately it was eclipsed by the 'Stang that appeared two weeks later. But there's no need to pity the 'Cuda. It subsequently got something the Mustang and Camaro for that matter could only dream of – the all-conquering, legendary "Hemi" engine beneath its hood.

And it was in the 1970s that Plymouth really got the Barracuda together. Now built on an E-body platform, it had the chassis it really needed to get the most out of its phenomenal power plants.

With its classic, hot-rod inspired, nose-down stance, the Plymouth 'Cuda looks like a drag racer and is definitely most in its element powering along in straight lines. At high speeds and on twisting roads it becomes a little too skittish and feels less composed than the Camaro, but in a straight line it's a hard act to beat and certainly faster than its heavier rival when the hemi V8 comes on full song.

However, all that power can get you into trouble, because the hemi's stiff throttle linkage is known to stick occasionally and bring all that grunt into play when you aren't expecting it – or least need it.

Chevrolet CAMARO Z-28

Inside Story

The Camaro was changed for the 1970 model, being longer, lower and wider than its predecessor. As before, it was a unitary design with a front subframe. The bolted-on front subframe carried the engine and front suspension pieces. A-arms and coil springs were featured at the front, while a live axle was suspended on leaf springs at the back. Z-28s got stiffer springs and shocks, front disk brakes and a thicker front sway bar.

POWER PACK

For the 1970 season, the SCCA altered the rules regarding Trans-Am powerplants. For the first time destroked engines were permitted for the race cars. Thus, the Z-28 discarded its 4950cc (302cu in) V8 in preference for a larger mill, the 350, albeit in LT-1 tune. With solid-valve lifters, lightweight pistons, a high 11.0:1 compression ratio and Holley 780cfm four-barrel carburetor, the LT-1 was rated at 265kW (360bhp) (gross) and a substantial 515Nm (380lb-ft) of torque.

Accommodation

Conceived as sporty 2+2s, neither car is big on interior space. The front buckets in the Camaro feel more supportive, but the 'Cuda seems to do a better job of space utilization, and its rear seat is certainly more welcoming than that of the Chevy. The Z feels more driver-orientated, however.

Handling

Even though it is a Trans-Am Street replica, the 'Cuda is outclassed by the Z-28. The nose-heavy Mopar tends to understeer, and the different-size tires do not really help matters. The Camaro feels more balanced and is much more controllable right up to the limit.

Plymouth CUDA AAR

Inside Story

Plymouth's pony car got a new platform for 1970, code-named E-body. This was essentially an all-new structure (though from the firewall forward it was the same as the bigger B-body). Like the Camaro, the 'Cuda carried a front subframe with an A-arm suspension, though load-bearing was by torsion bars rather than coil springs. At the back was a Dana 8¾ Sure-grip axle suspended by leaf springs. AARs got modified rear springs, resulting in a raked stance. Front disk brakes were standard.

POWER PACK

With the rules now permitting larger engines in the Street Trans-Am replicas, Mopar decided to use its 5572cc (340cu in) small block, which had gained notoriety powering A-body Darts and Barracudas. For the new AAR, Mopar engineers went to work, adding a stronger crankshaft and rods, plus stouter bearings and a special Edelbrock intake manifold, topped by three two-barrel Holleys. Output, for insurance reasons, was quoted at an under-rated 213kW (290bhp).

Performance

With more power on paper, it would seem that the Camaro has the edge, but in reality the 'Cuda, with its high-winding 340 and bigger back tires, is the faster machine. It accelerates to 96km/h (60mph) in just 5.8 seconds, compared to 6.4 for the more weighty Camaro.

Road holding

Despite its stiff springs and big tires, the 'Cuda is more at home on straight roads, and when things start to get twisty it tends to skitter and slide. The Z-28 boasts a slightly lower center of gravity and a finely tuned suspension set-up, which translates into greater security and stability on the highway. It is the hands-down winner here.

Ford THUNDERBIRD 1956

More power and a handsome restyle finally gave the Corvette the sportiness it deserved. Even so, is it really a match for the sporty, personable two-seat Ford Thunderbird, which outsold the 'Vette in 1956?

As traditional as "Mom's apple pie", the Corvette and Thunderbird are part of American culture – so much so that Don MacLean took his Chevy to the levee the night Buddy Holly died, and The Beach Boys got around in their girl's T-Bird until her daddy took it away.

Having your T-Bird taken away would be pretty devastating, because Ford's first foray into the world of two-seater sports convertibles is a pretty good response to the Corvette's challenge. It was only available as a convertible, and four seats would come later. However, a clip-on hardtop was a popular accessory to make it a bit more user friendly and comfortable than early 'Vettes.

The real jewel in the Thunderbird's crown is its torquey V8 engine. It creates less power but generates more torque than the Chevrolet unit, which means the T-Bird is only slightly slower across the range, despite its steel body weighing a lot more than the Corvette's fiberglass one. It's also a safer car to have an accident in, as steel is tougher than fiberglass.

What it lacks in performance the T-Bird makes up for with comfort and refinement. Combine its plusher interior with its softer springs and the Ford is the better long-distance cruiser.

FORD THUNDERBIRD

Engine Capacity	4785cc (292cu in)
Weight	1400kg (3088lb)
Power	150kW (202bhp)
Torque	391.8Nm (289lb-ft) @ 2600 rpm
Price	$3151

Acceleration:

0–30mph (48km/h)	4.2 sec.
0–60mph (96km/h)	9.1 sec.
0–100mph (160km/h)	23.0 sec.
Standing ¼ mile (400m)	18.0 sec.
Maximum Speed	178km/h (111mph)

Chevrolet CORVETTE 1956

CHEVROLET CORVETTE

Engine Capacity	4342cc (265ci)
Weight	1300kg (2870lb)
Power	156kW (210bhp)
Torque	366.1Nm (270lb-ft) @ 3200 rpm
Price	$2900

Acceleration:

0–30mph (48km/h)	4.0 sec.
0–60mph (96km/h)	8.2 sec.
0–100mph (160km/h)	22.0 sec.
Standing ¼ mile (400m)	17.9 sec.
Maximum Speed	199km/h (124mph)

Tired of watching European imports dominate the lucrative small sports car market, Chevrolet came up with the perfect homegrown alternative, the Corvette.

Not a muscle car in the traditional sense, the Corvette was pretty unusual in that it featured a hand-built fiberglass body over a regular steel chassis. So not only is it arguably better than the Thunderbird to look at, it's lighter too, and this weight advantage makes itself most apparent on the road. Climb behind the wheel of these early-generation Corvettes and you'll find a machine which is crude in some respects, but fun to handle. Once again it comes down to what you look for in a car; if you want something comfortable and relaxing to cruise over long distances, the T-Bird is best, but for some point and squirt, rough-and-ready action, the Corvette is the one to go for. Its leaf springs are less than ideal, but it's stiffer ride and tauter feel inspire more confidence than the Ford's when you're traveling fast and the road begins to twist and turn. Its steering wheel also has more "feel" than the T-Birds, so is the more rewarding driving experience. Both cars are now American icons. Of the two, the Corvette has the edge on looks, power, and handling.

Ford THUNDERBIRD

Inside Story

Swoopy, European-inspired looks hid what were essentially very standard American mechanicals. The original T-Bird rode a shortened Ford sedan chassis and, like its less glamorous brethren, boasted independent front suspension with short/long arms and coil springs, plus a live rear axle suspended by leaf springs. This, combined with the four-wheel drum brakes and softer springs for 1956, meant the car was more touring car than sports car.

POWER PACK

What made the Thunderbird a real hit, apart from its looks, was what lay under the hood. 1955 models relied on a 426kW (29cu in) Mercury Y-block V8 with 142 or 145kW (193 or 198bhp), depending if the car was standard or automatic. For 1956, power on the 292 increased to 147/148kW (200/202bhp), but the big news was the availability of a larger 312 V8, packing 158/165kW (215/225bhp). The larger engine was not available on cars ordered with a non-overdrive transmission.

Accommodation

Despite the addition of roll-up windows and inside door handles, the 1956 Corvette still feels primitive compared to its Ford rival. The T-Bird has a more comfortable seat and is more agreeable to drive over longer distances.

Performance

Both cars got a substantial power boost for 1956, though the T-Bird was also offered with a bigger engine. Despite having more power and less weight, Corvette, even in 154kW (210bhp) power-pack form, is not significantly quicker than the T-Bird.

Chevrolet CORVETTE

Inside Story

Apart from its fiberglass body, the Corvette was in many respects a conventional car, and many components were sourced from the GM corporate parts storage. The separate steel chassis carried an independent front suspension and a live rear axle. The Corvette had the leaf springs mounted outboard of the framerails to improve stability. The spring and shock rates were stiffened, as was the steering. As on the T-Bird, four-wheel drum brakes were standard.

POWER PACK

Chevrolet's magnificent 4343cc (265cu in) V8 made its debut in the Corvette for the 1955 model year and the vast majority of the 700 cars built were fitted with it. For 1956, the six was dropped and the Vette became exclusively V8-powered. Chief engineer Zora Arkus-Duntov developed a new high-lift camshaft for the 1956 model, which helped to boost power to a respectable 165kW (225bhp), enabling 0–96km/h (0-60mph) times of 7.3 seconds.

Cornering

At highway speeds, the T-Bird is a delightful yet relaxing car to drive; it is only when you push it that things begin to change. Tall tires and soft springs do not inspire much driver confidence. The Corvette, with its quicker steering and stiffer springs, stays more firmly planted to the road.

Braking

Stopping power was way behind other areas of automotive engineering in the mid-1950s, and with four-wheel drums, neither of these cars is quick to come to a halt, though the Corvette feels more sure-footed and fade is less noticeable.

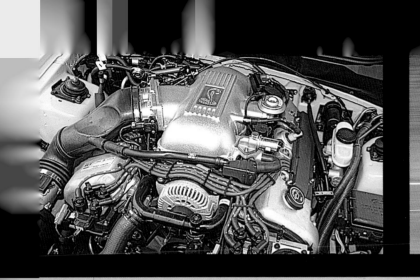

Sporting Adversaries

While it's true they don't make them like they used to, there is some mileage in the argument that they actually make them much better these days.

There was a time when driving a sports car meant putting up with all manner of quirks, idiosyncrasies, and inbuilt "character traits" that frustrated and lessened your sense of enjoyment. However, if you cast your eye through this chapter you'll discover a collection of cars that were unruly in their youth, but have now been reined in and successfully reinvented, and are virtually all now capable of being driven in daily use.

Take the Porsche 911. In its early days it had a reputation for being something of a wild child, but by the time the all-wheel drive Turbo came along in the '90s it had grown up into one of the most surefooted and capable supercars money could buy. And so it was with the car chosen to go head to head with it here. The Corvette Sting Ray slowly evolved into the supremely competent and more rounded ZR1 we all know and love. Progress, it would seem, isn't necessarily a bad thing after all.

But are modern sports cars really that much better than their beloved ancestors? The simple answer is that they are better in many respects, but not in others. Yes, they might lack a bit of personality in comparison, but you'll soon forget about all that when you climb behind the wheel and discover the difference ten, twenty, or even thirty years of advancements in technology makes. These cars offer speed, handling, and looks, but there's no trade-off for reliability and comfort. Perhaps more than anything, these cars prove that it is possible to reinvent the wheel.

Ferrari TESTAROSSA

Faced with the outrageous Countach, Ferrari took years to come up with something that looked as dramatic. Even then the Testarossa was heavier and lower-powered. Could it really match the older Countach?

Although it's not quite as way out or extrovert as the Lamborghini, the Ferrari is hardly a shrinking violet. Testarossa translates as "red head" in Italian, and is as much a reference to the cars fiery temperament as its red-painted cylinder heads.

Extremely wide and low, the Testarossa's looks, unlike the Countach's, are a help rather than a hindrance. The torquey, mid-mounted flat-12 engine generates an enormous amount of heat, so those massive strakes running almost the entire length of the car aren't mere decoration, they force vital cooling air directly to the engine

bay. Ferrari believed that luxury and practicality were almost as important to its customers as performance and handling, so the interior of this car is more user friendly and comfortable than the Countach's, which is a worthy consideration with both vehicles costing something in the region of $120,000 when new.

The ride is also less harsh and more forgiving in the Testarossa. And although it might be wide and heavy, it has an engine large enough to place it on almost level terms with the Countach. Even if it didn't, its looks alone would make up for any shortcomings.

FERRARI TESTAROSSA

Engine Capacity	4942cc (302cu in)
Weight	1667kg (3675lb)
Power	291kW (390bhp)
Torque	488.1Nm (360lb-ft) @ 4500 rpm
Price	$120,000
Acceleration:	
0–30mph (48km/h)	2.3 sec.
0–60mph (96km/h)	5.4 sec.
0–100mph (160km/h)	12.2 sec.
Standing ¼ mile (400m)	13.8 sec.
Maximum Speed	273km/h (170mph)

Lamborghini COUNTACH QV

LAMBORGHINI COUNTACH QV

Engine Capacity	5167cc (315cu in)
Weight	1446kg (3188lb)
Power	339kW (455bhp)
Torque	500.3Nm (369lb-ft) @ 5200 rpm
Price	$118,000
Acceleration:	
0–30mph (48km/h)	2.1 sec.
0–60mph (96km/h)	5.2 sec.
0–100mph (160km/h)	13.3 sec.
Standing ¼ mile (400m)	13.3 sec.
Maximum Speed	286km/h (178mph)

Few rivals are as bitter as Ferrari and Lamborghini. It was a dispute between Enzo Ferrari and Ferruccio Lamborghini in the first place that led to the latter building high-performance cars of his own. And few machines symbolize Eighties supercar excess like the Countach – a car that became a legend in its own lifetime, with its show-stopping looks and equally jaw-dropping performance.

Its name is an Italian exclamation of surprise, which the Countach still has the looks to elicit, while the Testarossa is almost conservative by comparison. Those 'scissor' doors became a trademark feature on Lamborghinis. Brutal and uncompromising, the Countach feels more like it was built for the race track than the road.

Under everyday driving conditions there is almost nothing to separate the two, so it's only on the track where a true comparison can be made. The Lamborghini has a marginally higher top speed and will reach it more quickly than the Ferrari.

However great the Countach looks, it's a terrible car in which to spend any length of time. With its tiny windows, bad visibility and offset driving position, it's a claustrophobic's worst nightmare – and proof that looks aren't everything.

Ferrari TESTAROSSA

Inside Story

Tradition still reigned: there's a separate chassis in square-section steel tube and wishbone suspension used all around. To offset the weight of the massive flat-12 engine over the rear wheels, twin coil-over-shock units are used on each wheel. The transmission is mounted under the engine, as in the Boxer. Those long side-strakes are more than styling devices – the huge engine needs them for its supply of cooling air.

POWER PACK

The flat-12 is an aluminum alloy to save weight, with 'wet' cylinder liners. Developed from the existing Ferrari Boxer engine, it is mounted over the transmission, raising the center of gravity. The revised engine has four belt-driven camshafts and there are 48 rather than 24 valves, fed by Bosch K Jetronic electronic fuel injection and putting out 37kW (50bhp) more than the Boxer. A dry sump oil pan allows the engine to be mounted as low as possible.

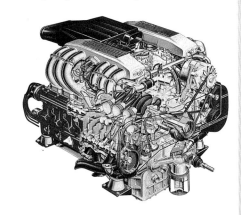

Accommodation

Countach's cabin is neither cramped nor claustrophobic; it's just a nightmare to get in and out of. Once in, you have to adjust to the offset pedals and impossible rear vision, but who cares? The Ferrari is more practical, better finished inside; Ferrari proudly called it "a 190mph [306km/h] living room".

Road holding

On dry roads both cars have phenomenal levels of grip, the Testarossa on its huge rear 280/45 VR415 Michelin TRXs and the Countach with its even larger rear 345/35 VR15s. You can lift off in a bend in both without disaster striking!

Lamborghini COUNTACH QV

Inside Story

A bewildering nest of steel tubes makes up the complicated but immensely strong Countach chassis. Much of the strength comes from the two massive fabricated sill sections. A much lighter steel frame supports the lightweight alloy body panels. The V12 engine is mounted longitudinally with the transmission towards the car's middle. Long trailing arms are used to augment the rear wishbone suspension, with twin spring/shock units per wheel.

POWER PACK

Designed by ex-Ferrari engineer Bizzarrini, the all-alloy wet liner Lamborghini 60-degree V12 had grown to 5.2l (317cu in) by the 1990s. Its 48 valves are opened and closed by four chain-driven camshafts, and it still relied on carburetors until the introduction of fuel injection in the late-1980s. Bigger than the Testarossa's flat-12, it also produces its power and torque higher up the rev-range.

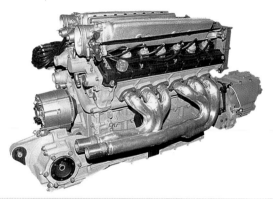

Handling

Both cars have quick, unassisted steering that's obedient to the driver. Performance is so great though, that you can only really discover there's power enough to get both cars' tails out with extra power in a corner on a race track. Ultimately, the lower and better-balanced Countach wins out.

BR 33

Ride

At low speeds, the Testarossa's big tires thump a little over bumps but it all smooths out at speed. Lamborghini knew no one would buy the Countach as a long-distance cruiser – stiffer sprung with much less roll through corners, it's surprisingly compliant.

Chevrolet CORVETTE ZR-1

Chevy's Corvette and Porsche's 911 are the world's best-loved sports cars, continually updated and improved. Is the ZR-1, quad-cam V8 Corvette up to the challenge of Porsche's 911 Turbo, with its four-wheel drive and twin turbos?

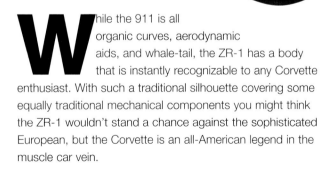

While the 911 is all organic curves, aerodynamic aids, and whale-tail, the ZR-1 has a body that is instantly recognizable to any Corvette enthusiast. With such a traditional silhouette covering some equally traditional mechanical components you might think the ZR-1 wouldn't stand a chance against the sophisticated European, but the Corvette is an all-American legend in the muscle car vein.

The ZR-1 is an incredibly involving and rewarding machine to drive. So, while the Turbo might be the ultimate incarnation of the 911, Porsche was obliged to add so many driver aids

and safety features to tame its wayward handling that it takes something away from the whole experience. The ZR-1 is the cruder, less sophisticated machine, but feels all the better for it. With a tendency to under, rather than oversteer, it's an easier car to handle at speed and should you push it too far, at least you're on familiar, more forgiving territory here.

Its reliance on simple technology has earned both praise and criticism. Some see this as a weakness. Others view it as a plus, keeping the costs of building the ZR-1 down and making it an affordable supercar. But it doesn't feel as complete a package as the ultimately more desirable 911.

CHEVROLET CORVETTE ZR-1

Engine Capacity	5727cc (349cu in)
Weight	1600kg (3528lb)
Power	300kW (405bhp)
Torque	522Nm (385lb-ft) @ 5200 rpm
Price	$68,043

Acceleration:

0–30mph (48km/h)	2.0 sec.
0–60mph (96km/h)	4.8 sec.
0–100mph (160km/h)	10.1 sec.
Standing ¼ mile (400m)	13.1 sec.
Maximum Speed	288km/h (179mph)

Porsche 911 TURBO

PORSCHE 911 TURBO

Engine Capacity	3600cc (220cu in)
Weight	1507kg (3323lb)
Power	300kW (408bhp)
Torque	541Nm (399lb-ft) @ 4500 rpm
Price	$115,000
Acceleration:	
0–30mph (48km/h)	1.5 sec.
0–60mph (96km/h)	3.8 sec.
0–100mph (160km/h)	8.7 sec.
Standing ¼ mile (400m)	12.3 sec.
Maximum Speed	290km/h (180mph)

Do you prefer a supercar to exhibit mild-understeer or wildly exaggerated oversteer when driven with enthusiasm? That would be the most obvious way to differentiate between the 911 and Corvette, if the 911 in question weren't a Turbo. The all-wheel drive Turbo is a technical tour de force that finally tamed the Stuttgart legend's unpredictable nature and eradicated its reputation for being dangerously tail-happy.

In terms of outright top speed, there's virtually nothing to separate them, but few cars hug the road as well the Turbo – not even the capable ZR-1, which can generate nearly 1g in corners before breaking away. The reason for this is that the Corvette relies on the traditional sports car layout with a big block V8 engine up front, driving the rear wheels, while the Porsche has a sophisticated drive set-up that distributes power to all four wheels for truly phenomenal cornering and handling ability.

Both cars can boast stiff sports suspension and breath-taking acceleration for a truly wild ride, but the 911 is one of those rare beasts – a true supercar you can use every day. You might have to pay more for the privilege – the 'Vette cost just under half as much as the $115,000 Turbo when new, but it doesn't feel as complete a package as the ultimately more desirable 911.

Chevrolet CORVETTE ZR-1

Inside Story

Tradition continued with the ZR-1. Like all Corvettes, it had a fiberglass body over a separate chassis with a big V8 engine driving the rear wheels. Even the transverse leaf springs (albeit in advanced composite materials) were retained, but in fact, the ZR-1 was a very modern car, with a six-speed transmission and cockpit-adjustable electronically-controlled shocks to complement the advanced, beautifully crafted, alloy suspension components.

POWER PACK

Since Lotus in England did the initial design work, Chevrolet carried on developing the ZR-1 V8, opening out the ports and improving cylinder head design to give 300kW (405bhp). An oversquare layout 10cm (3.9in) bore and 9.2cm (3.66in) stroke gave 5.7 liters (350cu in). Whereas other Corvettes had iron, single-cam engines, the ZR-1's was all alloy, with four chain-driven overhead cams and four valves per cylinder.

Accommodation

The Porsche interior is now very old-fashioned, the ergonomics poor, but the quality remains high. The ZR-1's interior is snug with a comfortable driving position. The electronic digital dashboard is a bit gimmicky, but displays info clearly and is part of Corvette's brash character.

Braking

There's little to choose between the two cars in terms of brakes. Both have huge vented disks all around and are more than capable of reducing from great speeds without fading. The ZR-1's slightly larger brakes give it the edge.

Porsche 911 TURBO

Inside Story

Double-wishbone rear suspension was added to the 911 earlier in the 1990s, replacing the old, flawed, and less predictable, semi-trailing arm system. To make the latest Turbo even more secure and capable of handling an astounding 300kW (408bhp) from the tail-mounted flat-six, Porsche opted for the four-wheel-drive approach first used on its Carrera 4. Like the ZR-1, the Turbo uses a six-speed transmission and enormous vented disk brakes, which are nearly as big as those on the ZR-1.

POWER PACK

Porsche's flat-six engine is all alloy and even more oversquare than the ZR-1's, with a 10cm (3.94in) bore and 5cm (2.99in) stroke to give 3.6 liters. Unlike the ZR-1's quad-cam, four-valve layout, there are only two valves per cylinder and a single overhead cam per bank of cylinders. This engine also has a small, intercooled, KKK turbo for each bank. That easily makes up for the ZR-1's larger displacement, helping to pump out 300kW (408bhp).

Ride

This is very good on both cars considering the performance, stiff suspension and huge low-profile tires. The 911 has the edge in refinement with better build quality and fewer creaks and groans.

Performance

There's only a totally academic mile per hour between them in top speed, but the weight of the Turbo engine over those huge rear wheels, coupled with 4WD means incredible traction. That, along with slightly less weight and a bit more torque makes the Turbo the winner in acceleration, but you would be hard pressed to spot the difference.

Mazda RX-7

By the early-1990s, Japan was producing some of the world's finest sports cars, but was the country's first supercar – Acura's mid-engined NSX – really worth $30,000 more than Mazda's twin-turbo RX-7?

Japanese engineers have a talent for showing the world how things should be done. Some would accuse them of copying and to a certain extent this is true, but the difference is that they improve on previous designs, taking on the good and ironing out the weak elements. So, like the Acura, the RX-7 represents a different approach to building sports cars, this time with an unconventional rotary engine mounted in the front end. Unlike the Mazda, however, the RX-7 was originally designed to compete in the affordable sports car bracket.

With its clever twin-turbo engine hidden behind its long sloping nose, the RX-7 boasts plenty of torque, more in fact than the larger-engined NSX, although it is slower by a few miles an hour and not as quick to accelerate.

With its power plant mounted up front the Mazda might not be as nimble as the mid-engined Acura, but it's still a solid performer in the bends and boasts high levels of grip. Although not as well balanced, it does feel more involving with all its power going to the back wheels, and that leads to a wildly exciting time.

When new, the RX-7 cost half as much as the NSX although it certainly doesn't feel half the car today. Proof indeed that sports cars can be reliable.

MAZDA RX-7

Engine Capacity	1300cc (79cu in)
Weight	1310kg (2889lb)
Power	174kW (237bhp)
Torque	295.6Nm (218lb-ft) @ 5000 rpm
Price	$29,000
Acceleration:	
0–30mph (48km/h)	2.2 sec.
0–60mph (96km/h)	6.5 sec.
0–90mph (148km/h)	13.5 sec.
Standing ¼ mile (400m)	13.5 sec.
Maximum Speed	250km/h (156mph)

Honda NSX

HONDA NSX

Engine Capacity	2977cc (182cu in)
Weight	1370kg (3021b)
Power	201kW (274bhp)
Torque	210lb-ft @ 5300 rpm
Price	$60,000
Acceleration:	
0–30mph (48km/h)	2.3 sec.
0–60mph (96km/h)	5.5 sec.
0–90mph (148km/h)	11.8 sec.
Standing ¼ mile (400m)	13.3 sec.
Maximum Speed	260km/h (162mph)

If you've ever wondered what a racing driver uses on days off, look no further. The NSX was built by Honda with input from Formula One triple world champion Ayrton Senna and was for many years the most expensive Japanese car available.

Designed to showcase Honda's racing technology and lure customers away from European manufacturers, the NSX was undoubtedly ahead of its time, yet retained the racing drivers' favorite formula of a mid-mounted engine.

Both cars handle supremely well, but the mid-engined NSX has the clear advantage here – it feels perfectly balanced and corners like it's on rails, while the Mazda has less feel through the wheel, which you need to hang on to as a result of its rougher ride at speed.

As well as being the better track car, the NSX is also the more capable road machine. Its sporty suspension offers a more refined ride under normal conditions. It has the classier interior, with more electrically operated gadgets and a greater sense of luxury. Not as exciting or exotic as some European supercars, the NSX is still a fantastic driver's machine, something that is never said of the Mazda.

Mazda RX-7

Inside Story

Mazda was after speed and handling perfection in a front-engined/rear-drive chassis, so the engine is set well back to give an almost ideal 48/52 percent weight distribution. The RX-7 is as small, light and as stiff as possible, with engine and transmission joined by a "Power Plant Frame". There are also stiffening braces on the high tensile steel body. The subframes carrying the classic wishbone suspension are also bolted rigidly to the body.

P O W E R   P A C K

Mazda put its Le Mans winning experience to good use with the twin-rotor RX-7 engine. Physically the engine is tiny but is the equivalent of a conventional 2.7-liter engine. Key to its power is the twin turbo installation. At high engine speeds the electronic control switches a valve in the exhaust system and the second turbo comes into operation, blowing through the first to give a compound effect. Two turbos are used so there's no initial lag as there would be with a single turbo.

Road Holding

The Mazda's 225/50 ZR16 Bridgestones and stiff suspension give immense grip, but the car's ride is badly compromised on poor roads. The NSX's even more advanced suspension gives much better road-holding characteristics on any surface.

Braking

The NSX has an outstanding braking system regardless of the speed. However, the lightweight RX-7 seems to stop more easily and quickly than the Acura.

Honda NSX

Inside Story

Honda – which makes the Acura – has the same aims as Mazda, but they used a different solution. Weight is kept down by using an alloy body, and a wishbone suspension design even more advanced than the RX-7's helps to maintain perfect suspension geometry through corners and over bumps. Even the suspension is made from alloy and mounted on alloy subframes. A more fundamental difference is mounting the engine behind the driver in the search for the ideal weight distribution and the ultimate handling balance.

POWER PACK

Acura's V6 has it all. Its block and cylinder heads are all alloy, with individual ignition for each cylinder; four cams; 24 valves; and variable valve timing. Once beyond 5800 rpm, different cam lobes come into play, giving higher valve lift and more high-speed power. More air is then forced into the hungry engine by the Acura's Variable Volume Induction System. The V6 just doesn't use a turbocharger; it will safely spin to 8000 rpm thanks to its titanium connecting rods so its relative lack of torque hardly matters.

Performance

Both cars get off the line together, but the NSX reaches 96km/h (60mph) a second ahead of the RX-7. Despite a 27kW (37bhp) advantage, the Acura is only 10km/h (6mph) faster than the Mazda.

Handling

You can change direction right to the limit. A flick of the wrist will put the RX-7 in a new direction without hesitation. NSX is as agile but more fluid to drive with better steering feel. Just think where you want to be and the NSX goes there.

Ferrari F40

Competition between Ferrari and Lamborghini is always red hot. Ferrari's V8 twin-turbo F40 appeared unbeatable, so Lamborghini countered with the Diablo and its huge V12 engine.

The rivalry that began in the 1960s and continues today between Ferrari and Lamborghini was represented in the early 1990s by the F40 and Diablo. Their fight for supremacy led to the creation of two of the Italy's most famous and lusted-after creations.

For the five glorious years in which Ferrari built the F40 it was the fastest, most powerful, and expensive machine in the world. And, as exotic as the Lamborghini undoubtedly is, the mere fact that it is more common counts against it.

Compared to the alloy and composite Lamborghini, the Ferrari is almost a featherweight with its Kevlar, fiberglass, and aluminium body panels. The interior is stripped for action too, with hollowed-out doors and carbon fiber race seats, so it's not as comfortable as the Diablo, although all that weight-loss means you feel like you're in a more dedicated machine.

The F40 was a development of the 288GTO race car and a showcase for everything that Ferrari had learned on the track. As such, it's the closest thing you can get to an F1 car for the road, and the most fitting way imaginable to celebrate the illustrious marque's 40th anniversary.

FERRARI F40

Engine Capacity	2936cc (179cu in)
Weight	1235kg (2723lb)
Power	352kW (478bhp)
Torque	576.2Nm (425lb-ft) @ 4000 rpm
Price	$415,000
Acceleration:	
0–30mph (48km/h)	2.3 sec.
0–60mph (96km/h)	4.6 sec.
0–90mph (148km/h)	7.5 sec.
Standing ¼ mile (400m)	12.8 sec.
Maximum Speed	324km/h (201mph)

Lamborghini DIABLO

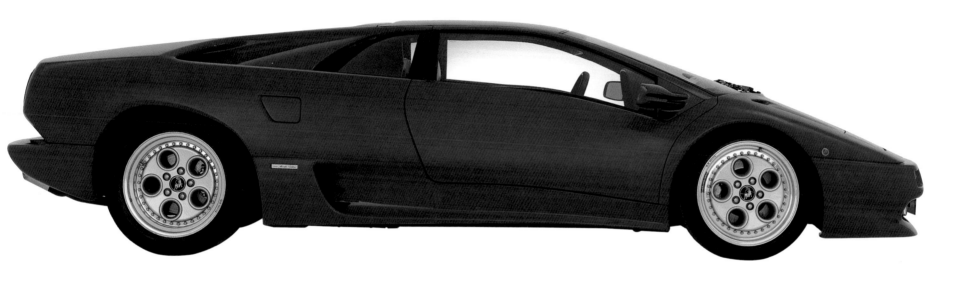

LAMBORGHINI DIABLO

Engine Capacity	5729cc (350cu in)
Weight	1576kg (3475lb)
Power	362kW (492bhp)
Torque	580.3Nm (428lb-ft) @ 5200 rpm
Price	$239,000
Acceleration:	
0–30mph (48km/h)	2.3 sec.
0–60mph (96km/h)	4.3 sec.
0–90mph (148km/h)	7.5 sec.
Standing ¼ mile (400m)	12.8 sec.
Maximum Speed	330km/h (205mph)

A bigger, better, faster, more usable Countach would be the best way to describe the Diablo. The name is a translation of the word "Devil", and with Lamborghini it was a case of better the devil you know than start again from scratch, which means its answer to the F40 has a similar outline to the Countach. It even retains the firm's trademark scissor doors and outrageous looks, but lacks the spoilers and outlandish add-ons of the earlier models and the Ferrari.

It might be the heavier machine, but the Lamborghini produces almost the same phenomenal amount of power as the Ferrari, and will match it almost to the second when racing through the gears, eventually topping

out 6km/h (4mph) faster than its rival at a staggering 329km/h (205mph).

In the company of almost any other supercar, the Diablo would look positively miserly inside. Its Spartan cabin doesn't even boast a CD player or electric windows, but is the lap of luxury compared to the stripped-out race-spec Ferrari.

The Lambo is the more useable car for regular road use, with servo-assisted brakes, electronically controlled variable shocks (on later 4WD VT models) and easier-on-the-arms power-assisted steering. It's also very nearly half the price of the F40, but most certainly not half the car for the money.

Ferrari F40

Inside Story

Cleverly mixing tradition and state-of-the-art design, the F40 uses a tubular steel spaceframe with carbon fiber and composite panels bonded to its lower sections to form an incredibly strong but light structure. The engine is mounted longitudinally behind the cockpit, driving the rear wheels through a five-speed transmission with suspension by double wishbones all around. The whole top rear composite section lifts up. The spoiler helps downforce above 200km/h (125mph).

P O W E R   P A C K

As you'd expect, the F40's V8 engine is something special. Cast in silumin, a light aluminum/silicon alloy, it has dry aluminum cylinder liners coated in nikasil – a hard nickel/silicon alloy – and shrink fitted to the block. Four belt-driven overhead camshafts operate four valves per cylinder. There's plenty of space for them as the 2936cc (179cu in) V8 has a large bore and short stroke to promote high rpm. Compression ratio is a low 7.7:1 to suit the twin intercooled IHI turbochargers.

Handling

The Diablo couldn't match the F40, the perfect tool for the most skillful of drivers, but adding four-wheel drive and power-assisted steering worked well.

Road holding

Huge 245/40 ZR17 and 335/35 ZR17 tires are the same on each car and give phenomenal grip on dry roads. Once water gets under them the sudden total loss of grip is devastating.

Lamborghini DIABLO

Inside Story

A bewildering mass of square-section tubes, in different grades of steel according to the loads imposed, forms the Diablo's chassis, and the steel roof is welded on to make a stronger, stiffer structure. The body is made from alloy or composite material and double wishbone suspension is used all around with twin coil spring/shock units for each rear wheel. The V12 engine is mounted longitudinally in front of the rear wheels with the transmission projecting into the cockpit area.

P O W E R   P A C K

Instead of using turbos, Lamborghini relies on the sheer power that can only come from greater engine capacity. It uses the V12 engine from the Countach, but the bore and stroke are increased to 5.7 liters. The Diablo's V12 is "oversquare" with bore bigger than stroke (9 x 8cm/3.42 x 3.14in) to accommodate the obligatory four valves per cylinder. Traditional chain-driven camshafts are used and a more precise engine management system permits 10.0:1 compression ratio.

Accommodation

The contrast is stark. F40 is stripped for action with carbon-fiber racing seats, and hollowed-out doors. In contrast, Lamborghini went the luxury route and fitted the Diablo with a fully trimmed interior and more compliant seats.

Performance

All credit to the Diablo; it weighs far more than the F40, yet with virtually identical power outputs, it's still a match for the Ferrari at every acceleration increment. As the cars hit 260km/h (160 mph), the F40's superior power-to-weight ratio begins to pay off.

Ferrari 456 GT

Ferrari went back to its roots with the 456 GT, switching back to a front V12 driving the rear wheels in a beautiful body. This is exactly the same approach as Aston Martin's big V8-engined Vantage. Who does it better?

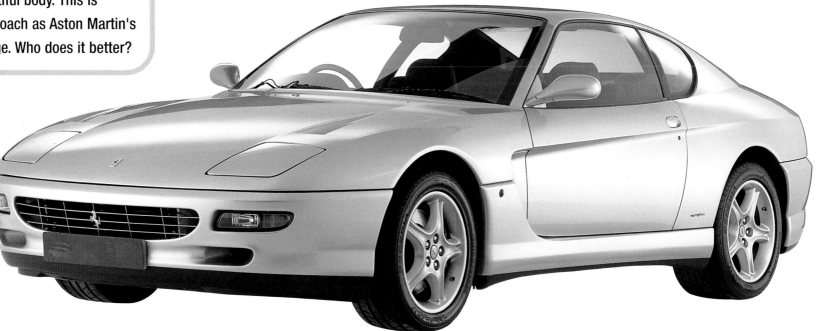

Amid-engined chassis might be all the rage again at Maranello, but Ferrari went for a front engine and rear-mounted gearbox layout with the 456 GT. It was a brave move considering the last Ferrari with its engine installed ahead of the driver was the poorly received (by Ferrari standards anyway) 400i.

The 456 GT was anything but poorly received, however. The Virage might be regarded as the ultimate incarnation of the Vantage, but to many eyes it simply can't hold a candle to the Ferrari. With its long sloping hood, short roofline, and cropped tail, it looks great when viewed from

any angle, and is visually very similar to the legendary Daytona 365 GTB/4.

Even though the Vantage is the faster and more brutal machine, the 456 feels the quicker and more nimble driver's car. Both cars possess excellent roadholding, but the Ferrari requires less concentration to drive it quickly, and tackles bends, corners, and hairpins like a nimble thoroughbred.

It all depends what you're after in a car: a fiery and potentially temperamental Italian or a traditional British powerhouse. Each will delight but in totally different ways.

FERRARI 456 GT

Engine Capacity	5474cc (334cu in)
Weight	1823kg (4020lb)
Power	325kW (442bhp)
Torque	747.1Nm (551lb-ft) @ 4000 rpm
Price	$275,283
Acceleration:	
0–30mph (48km/h)	2.2 sec.
0–60mph (96km/h)	5.4 sec.
0–90mph (148km/h)	10.3 sec.
Standing ¼ mile (400m)	13.4 sec.
Maximum Speed	310km/h (193mph)

Aston Martin VANTAGE

ASTON MARTIN VANTAGE

Engine Capacity	5340cc (326cu in)
Weight	1920kg (4234lb)
Power	404kW (550bhp)
Torque	539.6Nm (398lb-ft) @ 4500 rpm
Price	$217,600
Acceleration:	
0–30mph (48km/h)	2.1 sec.
0–60mph (96km/h)	4.7 sec.
0–90mph (148km/h)	9.1 sec.
Standing ¼ mile (400m)	13.2 sec.
Maximum Speed	307km/h (191mph)

Ferrari and Aston Martin boast two of the most evocative and well regarded names in sports car history. It was not by chance that they have created such a loyal fan base and reputation for themselves, and the cars shown here are pretty much representative of the breed.

Both machines have traffic-stopping looks and mind-blowing performance on tap, but are significantly different animals under the skin. The Ferrari, for example, employs the last word in tubular chassis technology, while the Aston is made from a traditional all-steel monocoque, so it's the stronger but heavier machine. That said, and despite its extra bulk,

the Aston is faster than the Italian in the race from 0–96km/h (0–60mph) and has the marginally higher top speed with its twin supercharged V8, even if it can't stay with the more nimble Ferrari in the corners.

The great thing about the Aston Martin is that it looks like a muscle car of old, with bulging arches, slab sides, and brutal lines. Handcrafted by traditional panel-beaters, rather than being honed in a wind tunnel, it's a more thuggish looking heavyweight cruiser than the delicate Ferrari. It also relies on the old muscle car standby, a large capacity V8 engine and gearbox under the hood, while the 456 has its six-speed transmission mounted in the back for better weight distribution.

Ferrari 456 GT

Inside Story

Even a car as new as the 456 GT still uses a separate tubular steel chassis, built at the Scaglietti coachworks and covered by Pininfarina's perfect alloy body, in the time-respected Ferrari manner. Another Ferrari tradition is the use of double-wishbone suspension all around, although these days, automatically varying shocks go with it. A new six-speed transmission is mounted at the rear to improve front-to-rear weight distribution.

POWER PACK

Gone is the flat-12 of the Testarossa, replaced by a new 5.5-liter V12. Naturally, it's all alloy; runs four cams and four valves per cylinder, but the oversquare V12 needs no supercharger or turbo, just the right cam profiles, electronic fuel injection, and a high compression ratio (10.6:1) to produce its 320kW (436bhp). The F550 shows there was even more to come from this engine; it boasts an extra 36kW (49bhp).

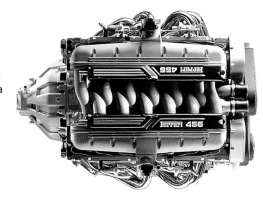

Handling

In the 456 GT, you can relax as it deals with roads or corners with perfect balance. The Aston requires concentration and is more suited to "point and go."

Road holding

Both cars have wide tires, and both offer huge levels of grip – although there's enough power to unstick them if you choose. The Aston's road holding is excellent by most standards, but it's not as reassuring as the ultra-composed Ferrari.

Aston Martin VANTAGE

Inside Story

Aston Martin used a steel monocoque for the Virage and now the Vantage, although the exterior alloy panels are non-load bearing. The supercharged V8 is mounted in the front along with its six-speed GM transmission (as used in the Corvette), even though the use of de Dion rear suspension means the transmission could easily have been mounted at the rear. The classic de Dion rear suspension is complemented by double wishbones at the front to help keep the 1920kg (4234lb) monster on the road at physics-defying speeds.

POWER PACK

Aston's muscular alloy 32-valve 5.3-liter V8 with its four chain-driven cams produced a healthy 243kW (330bhp) in the first Virage, but by adding two mechanically-driven Eaton superchargers, Aston Martin has blessed the engine with a vast increase in power. Power now peaks at 404kW (550bhp) when the short-stroke engine has reached 6500 rpm. The mighty V8 also produces a staggering amount of torque, an incredible peak of 747Nm (551lb-ft) at just 4000 rpm.

Accommodation

The leather interiors in both cars are comfortable and luxurious. The Aston has no flashy design to distract the driver. The Ferrari's interior, however, is more stylish but suffers in practicality – minor dials are out of the driver's line of sight.

Performance

Here, the Vantage scores big. There's nothing the 456 GT can do to rival the Aston's 747Nm (551lb-ft) of torque and the acceleration it gives. The Vantage is ahead of the 456 GT all the way, but both cars are astoundingly fast.

Aston Martin DB7

The 500SL's reign as the world's best luxury sports grand tourer has been threatened by the latest Aston Martin, the fantastic DB7. Can the sleek, six-cylinder Aston take on the might of Mercedes' superb V8 and claim the throne of the world's finest grand tourer?

There was a strong belief that Aston Martin of the late 80s and early 90s had perhaps rested on its laurels and reflected on its glory days for too long. The cars it was producing had become a little too bloated and almost a stereotype of themselves. Until that is, the new DB7 came along to shake things up.

With its sharp new look the DB7 was a shape that delighted when new and still looks great today, whereas the slab-sided Mercedes is starting to look its age and a little on the old-fashioned side. And it's the same story inside too. The

Mercedes is a high-quality car, but is far too businesslike and sensible for a sports car, and the Aston Martin is more adventurous in its choice of materials.

If you're going to spend this sort of money on a car then you'll want to enjoy sitting in it. Both the Aston Martin and Mercedes are big heavy cars in the luxury GT fashion, but the supercharged DB7 hides its weight better because of its superb handling. It also feels more modern and is the quicker car, turning in faster and responding to lighter inputs. Overall it has an undeniable edge over the SL.

ASTON MARTIN DB7

Engine Capacity	3239cc (198cu in)
Weight	1721kg (3795lb)
Power	246kW (335bhp)
Torque	489.5Nm (361lb-ft) @ 3000 rpm
Price	$125,000
Acceleration:	
0–30mph (48km/h)	2.2 sec.
0–60mph (96km/h)	5.8 sec.
0–90mph (148km/h)	14.8 sec.
Standing ¼ mile (400m)	14.3 sec.
Maximum Speed	253km/h (157mph)

Mercedes-Benz 500SL

MERCEDES-BENZ 500SL

Engine Capacity	4973cc (303cu in)
Weight	1890kg (4165lb)
Power	240kW (326bhp)
Torque	467.8Nm (345lb-ft) @ 4000 rpm
Price	$79,000
Acceleration:	
0–30mph (48km/h)	2.3 sec.
0–60mph (96km/h)	6.2 sec.
0–90mph (148km/h)	12.2 sec.
Standing ¼ mile (400m)	14.9 sec.
Maximum Speed	250km/h (156mph)

Like Aston Martin, Mercedes-Benz had been producing cars in its sport-light (SL) range that had become increasingly large and cumbersome, but the 500SL is still an extremely capable sports tourer. So, while Aston Martin decided to start afresh with an entirely clean slate, Mercedes built on what it already knew. The 500SL came equipped with a massive V8 engine and traditional Mercedes tank-like build quality.

Despite their heavyweight proportions, both cars handle like thoroughbreds with superb levels of grip in the corners and a magic carpet-like ride, although the heavier SL has more refined suspension and will happily soak up bumps and imperfections the Aston simply can't ignore.

Beneath its more solidly built bodywork the SL has something the DB7 surprisingly does not – ASR traction control. Get too carried away in the Aston and you'll need to work harder to win it back, while with it switched on the Mercedes is almost impossible to slide and the more forgiving and easier-to-drive machine on the limit. Whichever you choose, either makes a superb grand tourer with plenty to commend it, but the Mercedes feels as though it will stand the passage of time better, even if it dates quicker.

Aston Martin DB7

Inside Story

Layout is traditional with a front engine, rear drive and wishbone suspension all around. On the open-top Volante, the chassis was strengthened and stiffened compared to the coupe to compensate for losing the strength given by having a fixed, steel roof. The suspension setup was also altered. Wishbones are still used at each corner but the Volante loses the rear anti-roll bar and uses softer spring rates for the US market, where most will go.

POWER PACK

It's back to the classic Aston power unit; an all-alloy straight-six. Unlike the old DB twin cams this engine has four valves per cylinder and the air is forced into the engine by an intercooled Eaton supercharger. This gives power and low-down torque more typical of a much larger displacement engine. Whereas the old naturally aspirated DB6 4-liter engine gave 240kW (325bhp) and 532Nm (393lb-ft) of torque, the new supercharged six pumps out 246kW (335bhp) and peak torque is 489Nm (361lb-ft) at only 3000 rpm.

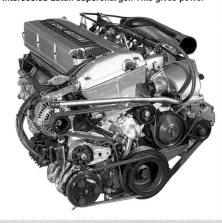

Performance

The supercharged Aston has more power, more torque and a better power-to-weight ratio, but the 500SL's larger V8 engine shows it's not far behind. On the road the Aston is faster off the line, and both cars reach top speed just over 250km/h (155mph).

Accommodation

Here the cars are poles apart. The 500SL is very business-like, which is slightly at odds with its luxury Grand Tourer image. It is quiet, refined and has an understated air of luxury. The Aston is more outwardly luxurious and more adventurous in its appearance and trim.

Mercedes-Benz 500SL

Inside Story

As is usual for Mercedes, the 500SL has a traditional front engine, rear-wheel drive set-up. The body has been designed to be incredibly strong, albeit at the expense of weight. Unlike some open cars, the Mercedes' body is so solid that it doesn't twist or shake at all, even over the roughest road surfaces. Advanced features include multi-link rear suspension, computer-controlled traction control and a hidden roll-over hoop that will deploy in three-tenths of a second should the car start to overturn.

POWER PACK

One of the great V8s, the 500SL's high compression (11.0:1) engine is all alloy with four chain-driven camshafts and four valves per cylinder. To make it even more responsive and flexible it uses electronically controlled variable intake valve timing. This system allows maximum smoothness at low engine speeds, optimum torque output at medium speeds (with its maximum 467Nm (345lb-ft) at 4000 rpm, it's 1000 rpm higher than the Aston), and maximum power output at high engine speeds.

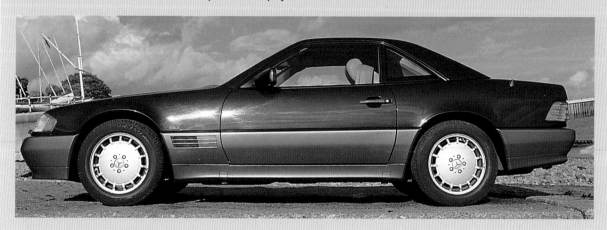

Braking

There's no excuse for poor braking these days and both cars excel. Following repeated stopping, though, the brakes of the SL start to fade while the Aston still stops powerfully.

Ride

The extra weight gives the 500SL the ability to ride smoothly over any surface. The DB7 gives a slightly stiffer ride, but even with its softened suspension the Aston can't match the SL.

Renault SPIDER

Two of the most advanced small sports cars in the world mark a breakthrough in design, setting new standards in agility and braking. Both are stylish and competitively priced, but which is better all-around?

Renault wanted something distinctive to get people talking about its sporting brands again, and got it in the form of the Spider.

Based on an ultra-modern chassis with a mid-mounted engine sending power to the rear wheels, the Spider might have been playing catch-up to the Lotus, with its forty-year head-start in chassis technology, but was a profitable car bolted together using parts drawn from existing Renaults.

Both cars are phenomenal on the road and track, but the French offering was built for the single marque Renault Sport Spider Cup racing series, so is the more dedicated racing weapon. That said, it doesn't handle as well as the Elise on the track, but is the better car for the road with its tuned suspension and softer ride. And, despite it's lack of roof and clip-on windshield, when the sun shines the Renault has the more comfortable cabin, with fatter seats, even if it doesn't have a heater or stereo.

Neither car is built with practicality in mind, but just climbing into the Elise is a difficult task, far removed from the ease of stepping through the Spider's distinctive gull-wing doors. More of a curiosity than runaway sales success, the Spider was only produced for a year and a half so is a rarer and more exotic machine than the Lotus.

RENAULT SPIDER

Engine Capacity	1998cc (122cu in)
Weight	955kg (2106lb)
Power	110kW (150bhp)
Torque	189.8Nm (140lb-ft) @ 4500 rpm
Price	$41,520
Acceleration:	
0–30mph (48km/h)	2.7 sec.
0–60mph (96km/h)	5.5 sec.
0–90mph (148km/h)	19.3 sec.
Standing ¼ mile (400m)	19.3 sec.
Maximum Speed	200km/h (124mph)

Lotus ELISE

LOTUS ELISE

Engine Capacity	1796cc (110cu in)
Weight	723kg (1594lb)
Power	87kW (118bhp)
Torque	165.4Nm (122lb-ft) @ 3000 rpm
Price	$33,500
Acceleration:	
0–30mph (48km/h)	1.9 sec.
0–60mph (96km/h)	7.7 sec.
0–90mph (148km/h)	14.8 sec.
Standing ¼ mile (400m)	14.5 sec.
Maximum Speed	200km/h (124mph)

I t's often said that if you want a car to go faster, you need to add lightness. It was a philosophy adopted by Lotus founder, Colin Chapman, for his legendary Lotus Seven and revisited for its spiritual successor, the Elise.

Sports cars had become ever more luxurious, complicated and heavy over the years, so the arrival of the Elise and Spider in 1995 marked a return to the basics. Both were similar in concept and purpose but there was no collusion between the two as they followed different paths to emerge at the same place. Both cars are feather light for example, but the Elise is the lighter, more agile machine thanks to its hand-finished fiberglass body, while the Renault is the

stronger and consequently slower car with its aluminum shell.

Like the Renault, the Lotus was designed to be a serious driver's tool with plenty of track-use in mind, but the Elise is the more user-friendly car for the road, with its roof and front windshield – which was a cost-extra option on the French offering.

Acceleration, braking, and cornering are all a little sharper in the Elise thanks to Lotus's chassis know-how, and its lighter weight. Taking into account the fact that it cost $8000 less than the $41,520 Renault when new, it is still a popular and well regarded performance car bargain.

Renault SPIDER

Inside Story

Like the Elise, the Spider's chassis is all-alloy but with square tubes welded into a more traditional-looking frame. In addition to being light it is both very strong and stiff, supporting an advanced double-wishbone suspension with compliance-free Rose joints (just like a racing car's), along with competition-style horizontal spring/shock units. The disk brakes were also used on the Alpine A610 built in the same factory.

POWER PACK

Power comes from a 2.0-liter 16V four-cylinder engine previously used in the Renault Clio Williams and also in the current Megane 16V. It is an iron-block, alloy-head, twin cam 16-valve design that loves to rev, reaching its peak 110kW (150bhp) at a high 6000 rpm. A relatively long stroke gives it a very reasonable 190Nm (140lb-ft) of torque, impressive for such a small engine and more than enough to get the Spider moving.

Ride

With its stiff bushings and thin seats, the Elise is hard riding, which can be tiring over long distances. The Spider is even more stiffly sprung yet Renault's engineers have tuned the suspension to deliver a much softer ride. Here the extra weight and slightly thicker seats come into their own.

Accommodation

Getting into the Elise is awkward. The seats are hard and there isn't any carpet. The Spider is also spartan, but the Elise does have the advantage of a heater and a top. The Spider doesn't have any creature comforts – even the windshield is an option. But these cars are for fun, not practicality.

Lotus ELISE

Inside Story

The key to the Elise's agility is its super lightweight chassis using thin alloy extrusions, bonded together for extra strength. It's not only amazingly light but extraordinarily strong and stiff. Weight reduction was of major importance to Lotus engineers, in an effort to achieve outstanding performance and balanced handling. The wheel uprights, front calipers and even the brake discs themselves are constructed from cast alloy (a first for a production road car).

POWER PACK

Lotus uses an existing engine for the Elise, the Rover K-Series four-cylinder twin cam, mounted transversely behind the cabin. Displacing 1796 cc (110cu in), it is also used in the MGF. As innovative as the Elise itself, it is an all alloy unit with wet cylinder liners, twin overhead camshafts and 16 valves. At 49kW (66bhp) per liter it's not the most highly-tuned small twin cam, but gives its maximum torque at only 3000 rpm and yet still thrives on revs.

Braking

Although it has larger discs, the Spider's brakes feel inadequate and stopping distance is too long. The Elise, on the other hand, has smaller disc brakes and benefits greatly from its light body design.

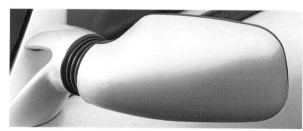

Performance

Weight is the deciding factor here. Despite the Spider's greater power (110kW to 87kW/150bhp to 118bhp) the Elise is lighter and as a result, quicker to 96km/h (60mph) by a couple of seconds. The difference in performance becomes even more apparent in the standing ¼ mile, the Elise covering the distance in just 14.8 seconds, while the Spider takes 19.3.

TVR CERBERA

TVR's brilliant Cerbera and the reborn Lotus Esprit prove that the British supercar is alive and well. Both offer willing V8 power, a refined chassis and razor-sharp handling, but which of them is the ultimate British sports car?

W ith their V8 engines and impressive handling it doesn't sound like there'd be much to choose between these cars at first, so the most obvious way to separate them would be to go on looks alone.

The Cerbera is arguably the more contemporary looking machine today, having been sculpted in the 1990s whereas the Lotus can trace its shape back to 1976. The TVR comes out on top in the interior here as well. It might look small on the outside, but its actually roomier inside than the Esprit, with comfier bucket seats, a more accommodating driving position and vastly superior visibility. And its dashboard is

more interesting to look at and better screwed together too.

The TVR's torquey V8 also creates the more sonorous engine note and it sounds fast even just standing in traffic. Hardly surprising, as it was originally designed to be used as a race engine and then tamed for use in a road car.

Both cars are undeniably a great thrill to drive, but the TVR has the more raw edge and more exciting ride. It might feel bumpier at normal speeds than the Esprit, but it compensates for this with superb roadholding, mindblowing acceleration, and charisma.

TVR CERBERA

Engine Capacity	4185cc (255cu in)
Weight	2000kg (2425lb)
Power	257kW (350bhp)
Torque	400Nm (295lb-ft) @ 4250 rpm
Price	$67,300
Acceleration:	
0–30mph (48km/h)	2.4 sec.
0–60mph (96km/h)	4.1 sec.
0–100mph (160km/h)	9.1 sec.
Standing ¼ mile (400m)	12.4 sec.
Maximum Speed	270km/h (168mph)

Lotus ESPRIT V8

LOTUS ESPRIT V8

Engine Capacity	3506cc (214cu in)
Weight	1346kg (2,967lb)
Power	256kW (349bhp)
Torque	433.9Nm (320lb-ft) @ 4500 rpm
Price	$71,500

Acceleration:

0–30mph (48km/h)	1.7 sec.
0–60mph (96km/h)	4.2 sec.
0–100mph (160km/h)	10.3 sec.
Standing ¼ mile (400m)	12.7 sec.
Maximum Speed	277km/h (172mph)

The design might be as old as the hills but there's no denying the capability of the Esprit. Despite trawling the dreadful British Leyland parts bin for door handles and other cost-cutting components, the Esprit was a rival to the likes of Ferrari and Porsche on the road, if not in terms of build quality, reliability, or kudos.

The TVR derives its name from Cerberus, the three-headed beast of Greek legend who guarded the gates of hell, and compared to the Lotus it handles like one. With so much power and no traction control or ABS to keep it under control, there's no way it can compete with the mid-engined and

wonderfully balanced Esprit. Lotus are justifiably renowned for their chassis know-how, and a few minutes behind the wheel of an Esprit V8 will reinforce this reputation. Smooth and unruffled around town, the Lotus feels just as refined and assured at speed. Corners can be taken at a blistering pace and it remains poised and easy to read at all times.

With a price tag of $71,500 in 1998, it cost rather less than a Ferrari but significantly more than the $67,300 Cerbera and, as good as the Esprit undoubtedly is, there's no getting away from its aging and therefore compromised design when in the company of the TVR.

TVR CERBERA

Inside Story

The Blackpool-based TVR company has always followed the same construction method, namely a steel spaceframe chassis clothed in fiberglass bodywork. The suspension is independent all around by wishbones and supplemented by anti-roll bars; there are gas-filled shock absorbers at the front. The brakes are huge vented disks with a 29cm (11.5in) diameter front and a 30cm (12in) diameter rear, but TVR deemed that an anti-lock braking system was not required.

POWER PACK

A small company, TVR has been very brave to develop and produce its own engines. The AJP V8 engine was designed by specialist Al Melling and is the first all-new TVR engine. It was developed for racing and adapted for road use, and is made of light alloy with twin overhead camshafts, in two versions: a 257kW (350bhp), 4.2-liter unit and a monster 4.5-liter with 309kW (420bhp).

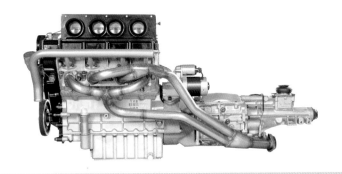

Accommodation

Being a 2+2 coupe, the TVR is the clear winner. As well as the small but useable rear seats, the front buckets are spacious, and driving position is near perfect. The Esprit's interior has a 1970s feel, the seats are uncomfortable and outward visibility is poor.

Performance

Both of these V8 engines have similar power outputs, but the TVR has more torque for low-down acceleration and is nearly 180kg (400lb). lighter. It therefore has a slight edge in acceleration over the Esprit.

Lotus ESPRIT V8

Inside Story

The Esprit has its roots in an Italian design prototype of 1972, which impressed Lotus so much that a modified version of it was put into production in 1975. The Esprit is mid-engined for ultimate balance and Lotus is renowned for its brilliant chassis. Esprit uses a double wishbone front suspension and multi-link rear suspension. Braking, as on the Cerbera, is courtesy of big vented disks (29cm/11.6in diameter front, 30cm/12in diameter rear) but, unlike the TVR, the Esprit has a standard anti-lock system.

POWER PACK

Although the Esprit started life with a 2.0-liter four-cylinder engine, a V8 introduced for 1996 has put the car in a new league. The 3.5-liter V8, developed by Lotus, is of all-alloy construction with four camshafts, 32 valves and two Garrett T25 turbochargers. It also looks great, with its red-painted cam covers and induction gear. Its 257kW (349bhp) is more than adequate, but, ultimately, it lacks the charisma of the TVR's AJP engine.

Handling

Both cars have great handling, although their approaches are different. Both are rear-wheel drive, but the mid-engined layout and better chassis of the Esprit ultimately gives it the edge, with near-perfect balance, minimal body roll and sharp turn in.

Braking

Both these cars have hugely powerful vented disk braking systems, but there is one crucial difference: the Lotus has standard ABS while the TVR does not even offer it as an option. While the Cerbera can be stopped in a very short distance, even in the wet, it requires a lot of pedal effort. In contrast, the Esprit combines powerful anchors with complete stability, safety and feel.

Panoz ROADSTER

The Panoz Roadster and the Caterham Seven HPC are from different sides of the Atlantic, but they have the same aim – unadulterated driving fun. Both have a top-notch chassis and are powered by two of the greatest modern engines.

The American-built Panoz takes obvious styling cues from the traditional Caterham/Lotus 7 but adds a few of its own unique and contemporary twists. It's a curvier and more flowing design than the Caterham, which if it has a fault, is that it looks like countless cheaper kit-car imitators, while the Panoz is virtually unique in its native country.

And it's not just the styling that makes the Panoz feel the more modern machine either. Both cars have a stripped-out-for-speed interior, but the Roadster is wider and better equipped. In fact, you can say it has equipment, which is not a statement you can make about the Caterham. It comes with leather seats, CD player and even air conditioning so feels more like a proper car than a go-kart.

Both cars have been honed for racing and are devastatingly quick, but the Panoz also has an unexpectedly soft ride when driving at regular speeds. The Caterham's suspension is simply too hard and uncompromising, while its rivals offer a better blend of practicality and performance. Ruthlessly fast and great fun to drive, the Panoz Roadster is ultimately the easier machine to live with, but at almost twice the price of the Caterham Seven HPC you'll have to pay a great deal more for your creature comforts.

PANOZ ROADSTER

Engine Capacity	4601cc (280cu in)
Weight	1115kg (2459lb)
Power	224kW (305bhp)
Torque	406.7Nm (300lb-ft) @ 4300 rpm
Price	$56,750
Acceleration:	
0–30mph (48km/h)	2.0 sec.
0–60mph (96km/h)	4.5 sec.
0–100mph (160km/h)	12.5 sec.
Standing ¼ mile (400m)	12.6 sec.
Maximum Speed	210km/h (131mph)

Caterham SEVEN HPC

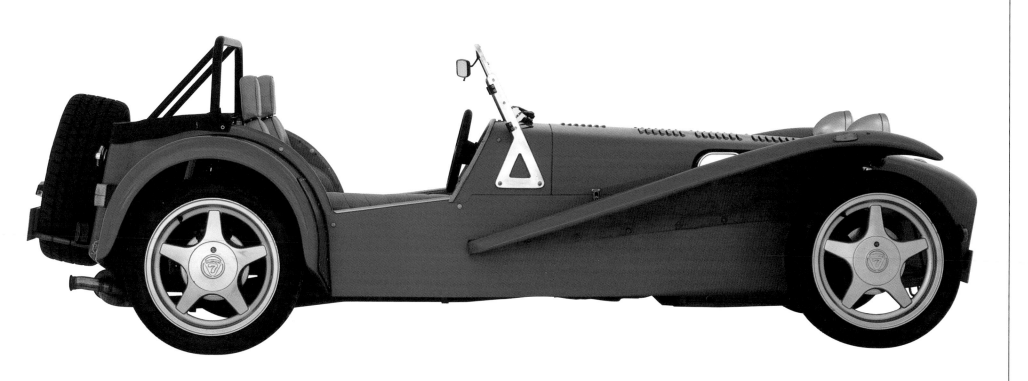

CATERHAM SEVEN HPC

Engine Capacity	1998cc (122cu in)
Weight	628kg (1384lb)
Power	129kW (175bhp)
Torque	210.2Nm (155lb-ft) @ 4800 rpm
Price	$29,208
Acceleration:	
0–30mph (48km/h)	2.2 sec.
0–60mph (96km/h)	5.4 sec.
0–100mph (160km/h)	13.3 sec.
Standing ¼ mile (400m)	13.6 sec.
Maximum Speed	203km/h (126mph)

Despite the name change, the Caterham Seven is still a Lotus 7 at heart. This lightweight, no-frills two-seater was originally designed and built by Colin Chapman before he sold the rights to Caterham, who continue to build it to this day.

Both cars look and feel pretty similar, but the Caterham has an old-school taste that classic car enthusiasts will prefer over the curvier, more contemporary Panoz.

Lower yourself into the cockpit of the Caterham and you'll see why so many drivers choose to wear a crash helmet. It's a vehicle built with a single purpose in mind and that's to travel as fast as possible. There are no creature comforts, just a rudimentary hood for when the weather turns nasty and no sign of a heater. Not that you'd feel the benefit of one – any hot air will be blown away by the wind the second you put your foot down.

Both cars boast rocket-like acceleration but the Caterham loses the battle only marginally, thanks to its less advanced aerodynamics. It is, however, the lighter and rawer car to drive so ultimately proves the most rewarding – if you can cope with its uncompromising character and utilitarian cockpit that is. It is a purpose-built machine for the dedicated driver only.

Panoz ROADSTER

Inside Story

The chassis for the Panoz originated from famous British race-car designer Frank Costin. Its has an aluminum tubular chassis frame and backbone to which are attached tubular steel subframes. Light weight is the aim, as evidenced by the high-tech superplastic-formed aluminum body panels – a technique derived from the aerospace industry. The original live rear axle is a Ford design for simplicity, while the wishbone front end recalls popular racing practice.

The V8 engine is taken straight from the latest Ford Mustang Cobra and continues Panoz' aim to make as much of the car as possible from aluminum, since both block and heads are alloy. With four camshafts, 32 valves, and fuel injection, the Ford 4.6-liter engine is state of the art and produces a massive 224kW (305bhp). It also has the benefit that it can be serviced by any Ford dealer.

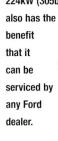

Accommodation

When you are trying to strip everything out to save weight, the last thing you expect is comfort. When you squeeze into the narrow cockpit of the Seven HPC you'll find absolutely no creature comforts – not even a heater. In comparison, although still spartan, the Panoz feels like a limousine. It is spacious and has leather upholstery, a CD player, and air conditioning.

Braking

These two cars are among the most powerful braking four-wheelers in the world. The Panoz has huge four-wheel vented disks – the front ones measure 33cm (13in) and boast twin-pot calipers. Ultimately, despite its smaller disks, the Caterham wins, however, because it has less weight to slow down.

Caterham SEVEN HPC

Inside Story

The Seven HPC is a direct descendant of the legendary Lotus Super Seven designed by Colin Chapman in 1957. Although the two cars have no common components, the philosophy of the design is the same: to be as light as possible. The standard Seven HPC weighs a mere 628kg (1384lb), thanks to its stiff and light tubular-steel spaceframe chassis with reinforcing aluminum-alloy honeycomb side body panels. Suspension is via wishbones at the front and a de Dion set up at the rear.

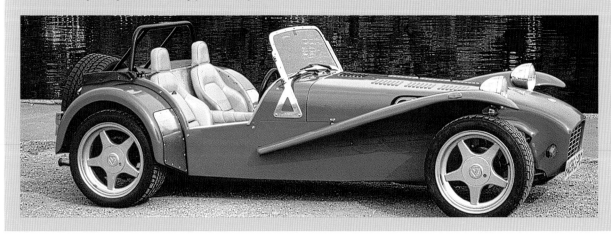

P O W E R P A C K

The HPC in the Caterham's name refers to the car's use of Vauxhall's powerful twin-cam 2.0-liter engine. Caterham has tuned the engine to take power output from the standard 110kW (150bhp) to a healthy 129kW (175bhp) at 6000 rpm by using two large Weber twin-choke carburetors and remapping the engine management system. It has a cast-iron block and alloy head that uses two-belt driven camshafts to operate four valves per cylinder via hydraulic lifters. The engine's redline is 7500 rpm.

Handling

For a pure rush of adrenaline, the Caterham simply cannot be beaten. The sharpness of its responses and the controllability of the chassis are unmatched. The Panoz is a sharp handler, but there is no contest.

Performance

On paper it may appear that the 224kW (305bhp) Roadster would destroy the 129kW (175bhp) HPC, but in fact on the road there is little in it. The answer lies in the Caterham's low weight, which is about half that of the Panoz. It storms to 96km/h (60mph) in just 5.4 seconds, not far behind the more powerful Roadster. The Panoz does score against the HPC, however, at higher speeds.

Nissan SKYLINE

It's a contest between two Japanese heavyweights. With dozens of racing victories, it is the more sedanlike four-seater Nissan, and not the stylish Toyota, that has the racing pedigree. But will that make it the winner?

They might not be the most exciting cars on the surface, but beneath the skin these Japanese offerings have the power and flair to ignite your soul, and more than hold their own in the company of seemingly more exotic machinery.

While the Supra is undoubtedly a fantastic performer, the Skyline GT-R is a hi-tech marvel and has a clear dynamic edge over the less advanced Toyota. A legend in its own lifetime, the Skyline notched up victory after victory in Japan. However, it earned further acclaim on the streets, where drivers would use its advanced four-wheel drive and clever power-diverting systems to their fullest possible effect in illegal drift races.

With perfect traction and an engine developed for touring-car racing, the Skyline's no slouch on the straights either. It will rocket off the line, and although not as fast as the Supra it's only fractionally slower all the way to 250km/h (155mph) and you get more feedback through the steering wheel.

Not that you have to rely on feel to get the most from the Skyline. It's such a predictable and responsive machine that its handling is totally at odds with its bland and ponderous styling which, it has to be said, is the big Nissan's only disappointment.

NISSAN SKYLINE

Engine Capacity	2568cc (157cu in)
Weight	1600kg (3530lb)
Power	204kW (277bhp)
Torque	294.2Nm (217lb-ft) @ 4400 rpm
Price	$80,000
Acceleration:	
0–60mph (96km/h)	5.6 sec.
0–80mph (128km/h)	9.1 sec.
0–100mph (160km/h)	12.9 sec.
Standing ¼ mile (400m)	14.0 sec.
Maximum Speed	250km/h (155mph)

Toyota SUPRA

TOYOTA SUPRA

Engine Capacity	2997cc (183cu in)
Weight	1562kg (3445lb)
Power	235kW (320bhp)
Torque	427.1Nm (315lb-ft) @ 4000 rpm
Price	$40,308
Acceleration:	
0–60mph (96km/h)	5.1 sec.
0–80mph (128km/h)	8.3 sec.
0–100mph (160km/h)	12.6 sec.
Standing ¼ mile (400m)	13.6 sec.
Maximum Speed	251km/h (156mph)

Even if the Supra's restrained looks aren't enough to get your blood pumping, its handling certainly should be. But if function always follows form for you, it's perhaps worth squinting a bit harder with the knowledge that it was loosely styled on the Ferrari F40 – you can see this in the rear spoiler detailing – so it's arguably a more visually stimulating machine than the sedan-like Skyline.

What it lacks in technical innovation the Supra makes up for with power and character. Perhaps not as interesting as some of its European competitors, the Toyota is a gutsy performer with plenty of power and low-end grunt. It's a superb machine for street racing with the traction control turned off, and being rear-wheel drive it feels predictable, chuckable, and huge amounts of fun. Body roll is kept to a minimum, and the Supra has the more refined suspension for everyday driving conditions, making it a comfortable daily driver.

The undoubted jewel in the Supra's crown is its phenomenal engine. It's a smaller capacity unit than the Nissan's lump, but kicks out a huge amount of torque. It's also super smooth and a tuner's delight, with plenty of scope for improvement. As fast and technically superior as the Nissan is, it just doesn't have the looks of the stylish Toyota.

Nissan SKYLINE

Inside Story

The Skyline is full of tricks, starting with electronically-controlled all-wheel drive. Speed sensors on all wheels, plus longitudinal and lateral G sensors, determine when torque (which is normally fed to the rear wheels) should be diverted; up to 50 percent can go to the front. At the rear, an active limited-slip differential varies torque infinitely between the two. More sensors also interact with the four-wheel steer system to determine wheel movement.

P O W E R   P A C K

Developed to race in the Japanese Touring Car Championship, the Skyline's power comes from a 2.6-liter straight-six twin-cam – a smaller unit than that used in the Supra. It also has four valves per cylinder, but since it has a short stroke of just 8cm (3in) the engine is much peakier, which means it makes power higher up in the rev range. The turbocharging system uses two Garrett T3 hybrid turbos, with lightweight ceramic impellers that work parallel and not sequentially.

Handling

As a big, superfast rear-drive coupe with conventional engineering, the Supra is about as good as you can get. It does lack ultimate feel through the steering, however. The Skyline GT-R benefits from race-inspired technology and four-wheel drive and grips the road like a true showroom stock racer.

Road holding

Huge tires (235/45 and 255/40), together with traction control, keep the Supra stuck to the pavement and provide great stability at high speeds. But the Skyline goes one better. The GT-R's high-tech all-wheel drive and all-wheel steer, combined with wider tires, result in almost unbeatable road holding.

Inside Story

Despite the hi-tech gadgetry, the Supra retains a traditional front-engine, rear-drive mix with the classic suspension format of double wishbones all around. But the old-fashioned approach ends there. Advanced construction makes the car light, and a front spoiler deploys automatically above 90km/h (56mph). Drive goes through a Getrag six-speed transmission, and a Torsen limited-slip differential at the rear and traction control help to keep the meaty rear tires in contact with the pavement.

P O W E R   P A C K

Toyota's straight-six twin-cam is a superb engine. Although it displaces a mere 3.0 liters, the combination of alloy cylinder heads, four valves per cylinder, twin sequential turbochargers and intercoolers produces an astounding 235kW (320bhp) and 427Nm (315lb-ft) of torque. It is silky and smooth, offering instant low-down response and tremendous zip from the turbochargers with minimal turbo lag. Without question, the Supra's straight-six is one of the most thoroughly developed performance engines.

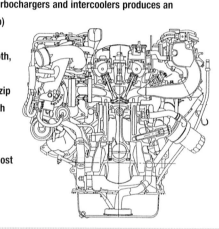

Braking

Both cars have superb braking capacity to match their extreme performance. The Supra's 28cm (11.7in) front and 31cm (12.1in) rear disks are all vented, gripped by huge calipers and assisted by ABS. It is a similar story in the Skyline, but the GT-R's brakes are light and lack feel compared with those of the Supra.

Ride

Both cars are able to strike a balance between taut cornering with minimal roll and offering a ride that stays acceptably comfortable over long distances. However, the Nissan is slightly louder and harsher at cruising speed, belying its origins as a roadgoing racer. The Toyota, as a true GT, is more refined, but has less suspension travel than the Skyline GT-R.

Pontiac FIREBIRD FORMULA

Since the 1960s, Ford and General Motors have staged the pony-car wars. Currently, two of the best are the Ford Mustang Cobra and the Pontiac Firebird Formula. Both offer V8 power, outstanding performance and value for money.

Who'd have believed the ponycar phenomenon would still be with us more than 40 years after its inception? But here it is, still kicking and still represented by two of its fiercest proponents, Ford and Pontiac, with their Mustang and Firebird respectively, still vying for supremacy with much revised and improved versions.

The Firebird was always a well respected and capable machine, but this, the fourth and final incarnation, is the fastest, most powerful model since Pontiac began producing them.

With its 5.7-liter engine, the Firebird has a larger capacity motor than the Mustang's hand-built 4.6-liter lump. This translates on the road to a Pontiac with more torque, low-down grunt and power than the Ford, but with only a hair's-breadth separating them while accelerating. The Pontiac is the faster machine by the tiniest of margins. Oversteer can rear its ugly head at speed, but when there's so much power available it's a risk you have to take. The Mustang can be just as frightening in inexperienced hands.

By the time the Firebird went out of production it was finally at the top of its game, whereas the Mustang was never quite as good as the first generation that kick-started the pony car revolution all those years ago.

PONTIAC FIREBIRD FORMULA

Engine Capacity	5.7l (348cu in)
Weight	1551kg (3420lb)
Power	257kW (350bhp)
Torque	440.6Nm (325lb-ft) @ 2400 rpm
Price	$24,500
Acceleration:	
0–30mph (48km/h)	2.2 sec.
0–60mph (96km/h)	5.4 sec.
0–80mph (128km/h)	8.2 sec.
Standing ¼ mile (400m)	13.6 sec.
Maximum speed	253km/h (157mph)

Ford MUSTANG COBRA

FORD MUSTANG COBRA

Engine Capacity	4.6l (281cu in)
Weight	1519kg (3350lb)
Power	224kW (305bhp)
Torque	406.7Nm (300lb-ft) @ 4800 rpm
Price	$27,000
Acceleration:	
0–30mph (48km/h)	2.3 sec.
0–60mph (96km/h)	5.4 sec.
0–80mph (128km/h)	8.4 sec.
Standing ¼ mile (400m)	13.8 sec.
Maximum speed	246km/h (153mph)

The fourth incarnation of the Ford Mustang appeared in 1993 and was produced until 2003, giving it the distinction of being the world's first and last pony car. (Tthe Mustang and its famous competitors are, however, currently being reworked for today's generation).

As usual, the snake badge makes all the difference. The Cobra was the ultimate performance version of the last of the old-school Mustangs, and boasted a hand-built engine for blistering performance, sophisticated suspension technology, and above-average build quality. You only needed to climb into the Mustang's better equipped and more carefully thought-out interior to reallize this.

Both cars wear massive 43cm (17in) alloy wheels, shod with meaty tires for superb traction and grip. Of the pair, it is the Mustang that boasts the better ride quality and feels smoother over bumps and uneven surfaces.

At the heart of both machines is a large capacity V8, which is put together by hand for the Cobra. Each produces boatloads of torque and impressive levels of brake horsepower, but the Mustang needs to rev to a higher degree if you're to get the most from it. The Mustang is also the pricier machine here, but is still great value for money considering its illustrious history, phenomenal performance, and undiminished popularity.

125

Pontiac FIREBIRD FORMULA

Inside Story

Introduced in 1993, the fourth-generation Firebird has come a long way since its 1982–1992 predecessor, but still relies on a monocoque chassis. The front suspension has been changed from MacPherson struts to unequal-length wishbones, although at the rear there is still a Salisbury live axle suspended by coil springs, and with a Panhard rod and torque arm to aid traction. Four-wheel vented disk brakes are standard equipment on all Firebirds.

POWER PACK

For 1998 the Firebird Formula and Trans Am received a brand-new V8 engine in the shape of the LS1. Like its LT1 predecessor it retains two valves per cylinder, but everything else, including the all-alloy block, is entirely new. This engine features distributorless ignition, 6-bolt main bearing caps, 1cm (½in) lift camshaft and symmetrical intake and exhaust ports. In standard trim, it is rated at 224kW (305bhp) and 325lb-ft of torque.

Road holding

The Mustang is better behaved on the road due to its front/rear weight distribution. The Firebird is more of a driver's car with better steering.

Braking

Huge four-wheel disks on both cars provide excellent stopping ability, although the Firebird, with its standard ABS, has the edge. Anti-lock brakes are available on the Cobra, but at extra cost.

Ford MUSTANG COBRA

Inside Story

This Mustang is based on the 1979–93 Mustang but with 40 percent more chassis rigidity. Known as the Fox platform, it has MacPherson struts at the front and a live rear axle. Compared to the chassis used on the previous generation of cars, the current Mustang features greater stiffening in the body and a standard strut tower brace. A pair of horizontally-mounted rear shock absorbers helps to reduce wheel hop under hard acceleration, but it doesn't have a torque arm running alongside the driveshaft.

POWER PACK

In 1996 the Ford Mustang received a new V8 engine in the shape of the 4.6-liter overhead-cam unit. The Cobra version has an alloy block and heads, with four overhead camshafts, 32 valves and distributorless ignition. Spark timing and fuel delivery are governed by Ford's EEC V management system. The peak power output of 224kW (305bhp) is produced at a relatively high 5800 rpm – greater than that of the Firebird's LS1 V8.

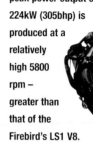

Ride

Despite its revised suspension, the Firebird is still fairly harsh and the live axle can be upset on bumpy roads. The Cobra has a more compliant ride and is far more agreeable on long hauls.

Accommodation

Compared to a family sedan, both the Firebird and Mustang have cramped interiors. The Firebird has more comfortable seats with better lumbar adjustments. The Mustang, however, has better outward visibility and driving position. In addition, the quality of the materials and location of the instruments and switch gear are superior to those in the Firebird.

Honda INTEGRA R

Adding a turbocharger to the Fiat Coupe produced one of the fastest coupes available anywhere. Acura's response is the high-revving Integra R, thrown into the battle without a turbo and with a smaller engine. Can it possibly compete?

It might look a bit like a sensible family car with a few gimmicky go-faster plastic bits strategically stuck into place, but the Acura Integra R is really anything but. Take one for a spin sometime and you'll discover it's actually one of the finest-handling front-wheel drive cars of the modern era, with plenty of low down grunt and a not unimpressive 230km/h (143mph) top speed.

Developed to compete in the Japanese sedan-car racing series, it was badged as a Honda in most parts of the world but called an Acura in the US, and offered a Far East alternative to Volkswagen's legendary Golf/Rabbit GTi.

Consistently in the motoring presses top ten driver's car listings, the Integra might be slightly slower and have to rev higher than the Fiat but it feels the more sporting of the two, and will outhandle it – and a lot of more expensive machinery besides – on twisty roads. To its credit the Acura is also lighter, better balanced and has stiffer suspension than the Fiat, so drives more like a race car than its blander looks would ever suggest possible.

Best viewed as a road car for serious driving enthusiasts who care more about function than form, what it lacks in charisma the Integra more than makes up for in feel and handling.

HONDA INTEGRA R

Engine Capacity	1797cc (110cu in)
Weight	1100kg (2427lb)
Power	143kW (195bhp)
Torque	176.3Nm (130lb-ft) @ 7300 rpm
Price	$24,500
Acceleration:	
0–30mph (48km/h)	2.6 sec.
0–60mph (96km/h)	6.7 sec.
0–100mph (160km/h)	16.9 sec.
Standing ¼ mile (400m)	15.2 sec.
Maximum speed	230km/h (143mph)

Fiat COUPE

FIAT COUPE

Engine Capacity	1998cc (122cu in)
Weight	1345kg (2966lb)
Power	162kW (220bhp)
Torque	309.1Nm (228lb-ft) @ 2500 rpm
Price	$33,990
Acceleration:	
0–30mph (48km/h)	2.7 sec.
0–60mph (96km/h)	6.5 sec.
0–100mph (160km/h)	14.7 sec.
Standing ¼ mile (400m)	14.7 sec.
Maximum speed	250km/h (155mph)

Cast your eye over the Fiat Coupe and you'll no doubt agree that it's a great looking car. With it's drooping nose, faired-in, bulging headlights and distinctive slashes in its flanks, it looks like a vastly more exotic offering from one of Fiat's more upmarket country cousins, and yet it cost just $33,990 when new.

With 162kW (220bhp) on tap, this is a veritable pocket rocket with the "go" to match its "show," despite relying on an existing Fiat chassis and parts-bin running gear. It also deals admirably with the apparent handicap of being front-wheel drive, so has a tendency to understeer rather than oversteer if pushed hard.

Designed as a compromise between comfort and sportiness, the Fiat looks as good on the inside as it does outside. It's stylish, rapid, and torquey enough to out-accelerate and go on to a higher top speed than the Integra, but doesn't feel as solid, planted, or chuckable.

Step inside and you'll forget about any misgivings you might have had. Thanks to input from Pininfarina, the Coupe has the more stylish dashboard and cockpit, with a body-colored metal section to brighten things up and inject some personality, which the Integra's cockpit is totally lacking in. What it all boils down to is preference. Do you want Italian passion or Japanese know-how?

Honda INTEGRA R

Inside Story

The R stands for Racing. Thus the Integra has a very rigid chassis with four braces added to increase stiffness. The double wishbone suspension for all four wheels uses stiffer springs and shock absorbers. Unnecessary equipment is removed to make the R as light as possible and the five-speed transmission on the transverse four has very short ratios (top gives only 29km/h [18mph]/1000 rpm) to increase acceleration, but the R is not quite as front-heavy as the Fiat.

POWER PACK

The Acura's power is produced without a turbo thanks to its well proven VTEC variable valve timing, which gives it a second wind beyond 6000 rpm where most engines are gasping. It means the small 1.8-liter all-alloy twin-cam four, with its 16 lightweight valves, fuel-flowed head and a crankshaft as perfectly balanced as a race car engine's, produces its outstanding 143kW (195bhp) maximum power at a high 8000 rpm and can rev to 9000 rpm.

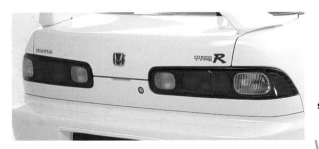

Handling

On paper the Acura should be a clear winner. It has less weight over the front wheels and a superior suspension design of double wishbones. The whole car is also lighter, which makes it more agile. These advantages give the Acura the edge, and its stiffer suspension means less cornering roll and lets the driver exploit the car's dynamics.

Road holding

With its 205/50 ZR16 Pirelli P-Zeros, the Fiat puts more rubber on the road than the Acura with its slightly smaller 195/55 ZR15 Bridgestone Potenzas, but virtually all the advantage is taken up by the Coupe's greater weight. The Integra R makes more efficient use of its rubber thanks to excellent wheel control.

Fiat COUPE

Inside Story

Fiat's Coupe is based on the Bravo/Brava family car's floorpan with MacPherson strut front and trailing arm rear suspension, stiff anti-roll bars at each end and quick-ratio rack-and-pinion steering. The engine is transversely mounted, driving the front wheels through a five-speed transmission. With so much power on tap, top gear is a high ratio and gives a relaxed 40km/h (25mph) per 1000rpm. Its iron-block five-cylinder engine plus turbo gives it a markedly front-heavy (68:32) weight distribution.

POWER PACK

The Fiat's engine is a short-stroke twin-cam and has four valves per cylinder. It is a step beyond most 2.0-liter twin-cam engines since it has five cylinders. Although in-line five engines are better than in-line fours, they are not as smooth as a six. The Fiat's is therefore fitted with twin contra-rotating balancer shafts to help reduce the vibration. It is the intercooled turbocharger that really gives the outstanding power and torque output, however.

Performance

There should be no contest between a 2.0-liter turbo and a normally aspirated 1.8-liter, and it's a credit to the Acura's race-tuned and frantically-revving four that it comes as close to matching the blown Fiat as it does. The gap stretches to a few seconds by 160km/h (100mph), due to the Coupe's massive torque advantage.

Ride

The Acura's stiff, uncompromising set-up makes the car skitter about with the driver feeling every bump; the bigger it is the worse it feels. In contrast, the Coupe has softer springs and shock absorbers, which give a smoother ride. This is at the expense of more roll and, as the seats are softer than the Acura's rigid Recaros, the overall effect is exaggerated.

Maserati GHIBLI CUP

For years the idea that a Maserati could rival a BMW, let alone the M3 – a car known as one of the world's best performers in its class – was absurd. But could it be that the M3 met its match with the Ghibli Cup?

You might not realize by looking at it, but with its twin turbocharged V6 engine the Maserati Ghibli Cup had the highest power output per liter of any street-legal car, giving it more power than the likes of the Jaguar XJ220 and mighty Bugatti EB110. So, while the M3 is certainly no slouch – it has a top-speed limited to just 220km/h (137mph) – the Maserati will rocket on to a highly illegal 272km/h (169mph) and hit 160km/h (100mph) in just 13 seconds once the turbochargers come on song.

It can handle the corners too. With its short wheelbase, massive tires, and direct steering the Ghibli is more fun to drive than the BMW. It boasts a huge amount of grip, as well

as more traction, and with so much power on tap, supplies of controllable oversteer are never very far away should you decide that you want it.

Built with luxury as well as performance in mind, the Maserati might not be as well screwed together or as comfortable as the Germanic offering, but it certainly looks the part, and its interior hints at where the extra money required to buy one new went. The Ghibli Cup and M3 are two very different animals built for the same purpose. Which you prefer depends on whether you value looks or efficiency more. Follow your heart and the Maserati wins.

MASERATI GHIBLI CUP

Engine Capacity	1996cc (122cu in)
Weight	1424kg (3140lb)
Power	243kW (330bhp)
Torque	379.6Nm (280lb-ft) @ 4000 rpm
Price	$66,800
Acceleration:	
0–60mph (96km/h)	5.5 sec.
0–80mph (128km/h)	9.0 sec.
0–100mph (160km/h)	13.5 sec.
Standing ¼ mile (400m)	14.4 sec.
Maximum speed	272km/h (169mph)

BMW M3

B M W   M 3

Engine Capacity	3152cc (192cu in)
Weight	1440kg (3175lb)
Power	176kW (240bhp)
Torque	320Nm (236 lb-ft) @ 3800 rpm
Price	$39,280
Acceleration:	
0–60mph (96km/h)	5.5 sec.
0–80mph (128km/h)	8.9 sec.
0–100mph (160km/h)	13.0 sec.
Standing ¼ mile (400m)	14.0 sec.
Maximum speed	220km/h (137mph)

The BMW 3-Series has long been the benchmark against which all other compact sporting sedans are judged. The M3 version is the incredibly popular potent variant.

It might look like an everyday sedan car, but looks are deceptive where the M3 is concerned. With handling that can embarrass many a so-called supercar, it is still a vehicle you can use every day. The Ghibli, on the other hand, feels more delicate and likely to break, with its poorer build quality and more temperamental nature. The BMW is also more comfortable than the very upright and awkward Maserati,

with a driving position that is as near perfect as they come.

The Maserati is ultimately faster than the BMW, but from standstill to 160km/h (100mph) the M3 is the quicker, so under normal driving conditions accolades must go to the Germans. And the BMW's longer wheelbase and advanced suspension mean it is easily a match for the technically clever Maserati in the corners. So, despite the massive price discrepancy, the M3 never fails to impress. On paper and perhaps even in the metal, the Ghibli might appear the more exciting prospect, but ultimately the BMW is the more efficient and effective driving machine.

Maserati GHIBLI CUP

Inside Story

Maserati retains a conventional layout for the Ghibli, with the V6 driving the rear wheels through a six-speed Getrag transmission. Given how well it performs, the suspension design sounds ordinary, with MacPherson struts and an anti-roll bar at the front and semi-trailing arms at the rear. Lowered and stiffened, this set up works perfectly in the Ghibli, as does the precise rack-and-pinion steering, which takes just three turns lock to lock.

POWER PACK

Simply one of the most incredible engines in production, it is a small all-alloy 2.0-liter V6 with a short-stroke, four overhead cams and four valves per cylinder. What makes it so remarkable is the effect of the two small Japanese IHI turbochargers, each with their own dedicated intercooler, pumping air into the 7.6:1-compression engine to produce 121kW (165bhp) per liter. That is more power than any other road engine, Ferrari's finest included.

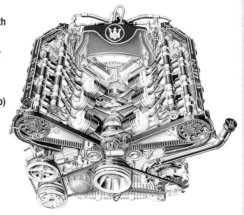

Handling

The short wheelbase and direct steering make the Ghibli Cup a revelation. Turning into corners is sharp despite all the power available, while oversteer is easily controlled. Maserati's wonderful steering and greater fun factor becomes more appealing here.

Braking

Racing development means the Ghibli Cup's big Brembo calipers and vented four-wheel disks are outstanding, progressive and fade-free. The M3 has larger front disks, which are more than adequate for any task a driver can throw at them.

Inside Story

The M3 still uses the classic BMW recipe – a straight-six engine at the front driving the rear wheels. In this case it is through a five-speed manual transmission. One of BMW's greatest advances in recent years is the rear suspension, with the multi-link system being so much better than the previous semi-trailing arms. MacPherson struts and an anti-roll bar are used at the front, along with a rack-and-pinion steering system that has 3.25 turns, lock to lock. The M3 is longer than the Ghibli and has a longer wheelbase.

POWER PACK

Also one of the great engines, BMW's straight-six is an iron-block, alloy-head design with double overhead camshafts and four valves per cylinder. It revs high with maximum power at 7400 rpm despite its relatively long stroke. Its revving ability comes from an advanced variable valve timing on both intake and exhaust valves, rather than most other designs where it's usually just the intake valves. The effect is noticeable, first at around 2500 rpm, and continues to pull through.

Accommodation

Here is a clear win for the M3 because its driving position is nearly perfect. The Ghibli's is flawed with a very upright and uncomfortable driving position.

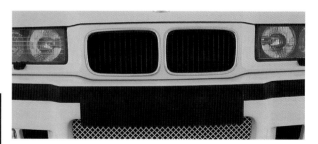

Road holding

On paper the M3 should have the advantage; its longer wheelbase and perfect weight distribution should help stability and ultimate lateral g. Although it does, the front-heavy, short-wheelbase Ghibli feels more secure.

Buick GNX

Buick's GNX was unquestionably the meanest and fastest-accelerating muscle car of the 1980s, but how does it compare to the fearsome 1993 Cobra R, a highly tuned Mustang built purely for competition?

The clean-cut American hero against the mean and moody new kid on the block is a pretty flowery, yet accurate, way to sum up these iconic muscle machines.

Based on the Regal Grand National, the Buick GNX was the muscle car of the 1980s, as well as being General Motors' fastest ever production sedan. Pop the hood on either vehicle and you'll find some pretty potent machinery – a V8 in the Ford and a turbo-charged V6 in the Buick. On paper the GNX looks like it might have its work cut out against the Mustang, as it has the smaller capacity and less impressive top speed – just 200km/h (124mph) as opposed to the Mustang's 245km/h

(152mph) – but, thanks to the supercharger it produces more horsepower and the quicker acceleration time.

It's pretty good inside too. Whereas the Cobra R was built to go racing, the GNX has a more spacious and comfortable cabin with plenty of toys to keep you and the entire family entertained on long trips. They'd have to stay at home if you bought the stripped-out Mustang, because it's so basic inside that it doesn't even have a rear seat.

Made for just one year only, a little more than 500 were built so the chances of finding one of Detroit's rarest and most collectable vehicles are sadly now pretty slim.

BUICK GNX

Engine Capacity	3785cc (231cu in)
Weight	1608kg (3545lb)
Power	203kW (276bhp)
Torque	488.1Nm (360lb-ft) @ 2400 rpm
Price	$29,290
Acceleration:	
0–30mph (48km/h)	2.1 sec.
0–60mph (96km/h)	5.5 sec.
0–100mph (160km/h)	17.0 sec.
Standing ¼ mile (400m)	13.4 sec
Maximum speed	199km/h (124mph)

Ford MUSTANG COBRA R

FORD MUSTANG COBRA R

Engine Capacity	4948cc (302cu in)
Weight	1482kg (3268lb)
Power	173kW (235bhp)
Torque	406.7Nm (300lb-ft) @ 3000 rpm
Price	$25,692
Acceleration:	
0–30mph (48km/h)	2.3 sec.
0–60mph (96km/h)	5.8 sec.
0–100mph (160km/h)	17.1 sec.
Standing ¼ mile (400m)	14.0 sec.
Maximum speed	245km/h (152mph)

A stock car straight from the showroom, the Cobra R is the epitome of the 1979 'Fox' platform-based Mustang. If you thought the Buick was a limited edition then think again, because only 107 Mustang Cobra Rs rolled out of the factory and all of them were sold before production even got under way. You want rare? You got it.

While the Buick panders to the sort of driver who wants comfort and things like a radio, the Mustang laughs at such unnecessary trinkets. Everything in this car is geared toward speed, so if it didn't need it or it slowed it down to keep it, it

didn't go in. Uncomfortable, impractical, and a bit extreme maybe, but the Cobra R feels all the more interesting for it.

In a straight line the GNX proves to be a fine car, but introduce it to a corner and it embarrasses itself in front of the stiffer and more poised Ford. In fact, its huge wheels and massive tires make it one of the finest-cornering Mustangs ever produced.

Modern muscle doesn't come any more dedicated or harder to come by than either of these two, but if you want the ultimate, with no compromise, then the better-built and ultimately more involving Mustang Cobra R has to be the option to go for.

Buick GNX

Inside Story

The GNX shares it chassis with the base Regals and Grand Nationals. It's built on a separate body/chassis with unequal-length wishbones and coil springs at the front, plus a live, 3.42:1-geared positraction rear axle and coils out back. Sideloads are absorbed by a Panhard rod while a stiff torque arm provides better traction off the line. These items are unique to the GNX. It uses the same 19mm (¾in) anti-roll bar and Delco shock absorbers found in the GN.

POWER PACK

Eschewing the traditional Detroit approach of "bigger is better" toward hot rodding, the GNX uses a version of Buick's turbocharged 3785cc (231cu in) V6. This engine first appeared in 1976 and was an option on Regals starting in 1978. Although it made a formidable 180kW (245bhp) in 1987 T-Types and GNs, engineers installed an uprated ECM, modified intercooler and lightweight ceramic impeller in the Garrett T3 turbocharger. The result was 203kW (276bhp) at 4400 rpm.

Accommodation

Cobra Rs were built strictly for racing, and the absence of a radio, A/C and back seat severely compromises practicality. The GNX, on the other hand, has comfortable seats and a roomy cabin, making it a good daily driver.

Performance

The Cobra is a quick car to drive, with a rev-happy yet torquey motor. However, the GNX has the clear advantage – 30kW (41bhp) more, plus a modified turbo and recalibrated ECM, giving it the edge in acceleration.

Ford MUSTANG COBRA R

Inside Story

1993 marked the final iteration of the "Fox" chassis. Riding on a 255cm (100.5in) wheelbase, the Cobra R has modified MacPherson strut front suspension, with a live axle, coils and trailing arms at the rear. Bred for SCCA showroom stock road racing, Cobra Rs have thicker sway bars than standard 5.0Ls, plus softer Eibach springs (for improved traction), gas-pressurized Koni shocks, with an extra pair of horizontal rear shocks and four-wheel disk brakes.

POWER PACK

Until 1995, the standard Mustang performance engine was the venerable Ford 4950cc (302cu in) small-block V8. In 1993, the standard 5.0-liter was rated at 151kW (205bhp), but for the Cobra, Ford's Special Vehicle Team added a few additional tweaks, such as a larger cast aluminum Ford Motorsport intake and GT-40 cylinder heads to boost power up to 173kW (235bhp). It has a higher flow fuel pump, larger fuel injectors and a recalibrated computer.

Road holding

Again, the Cobra gets the nod. The GNX's separate chassis and less sophisticated suspension design make it a handful, and with so much power, oversteer is easy to provoke.

Braking

Fitted with monster four-wheel disks (vented at the front) plus dual-piston calipers, the Cobra R is far superior to the Buick when it comes to stopping, taking fewer than 44m (143ft) to come to a complete standstill. The GNX, by virtue of its smaller front disks and rear drums, goes from 96km/h (60mph) to rest in 47m (155ft).

Mercedes-Benz 560 SL

Cadillac's ultra-luxury 1987 Allanté got more than its fair share of controversy when it was launched. In reality, however, is it a worthy competitor for the car it was aimed at, the fast and exclusive 1987 Mercedes-Benz 560SL?

The "Sport Light" range has been a staple part of the Mercedes line-up since 1954 when the name was first applied to its legendary predecessor, the Gullwing. The name itself is a misnomer because these cars are more luxurious than sporting and tip the scales at a weighty 1619kg (3570lb), so hardly qualify as "light" either.

There is, however, a timeless elegance about these stylish and very capable machines, and when it was current, the 560 SL set the benchmark against which all other luxury roadsters were judged. So, as accomplished and exotic as the Cadillac is, it is outgunned and outclassed at every turn by the Teutonic tourer.

While the Cadillac's styling courted controversy, the Mercedes has always attracted admiring comments about its engineering excellence, impressive performance, and quality interior. The moment you climb inside an SL you know you're in a better machine than the Cadillac. It has more supportive seats, is made from superior materials and creates a greater sense of occasion.

Designed specifically to appeal to the American market, the 560 SL was the ultimate incarnation of the R107/W116 design and is the better car in every respect.

MERCEDES-BENZ 560 SL

Engine Capacity	5.6l (342cu in)
Weight	1619kg (3570lb)
Power	167kW (227bhp)
Torque	378.3Nm (279lb-ft) @ 3250 rpm
Price	$55,300
Acceleration:	
0–30mph (48km/h)	3.1 sec.
0–60mph (96km/h)	8.0 sec.
0–100mph (160km/h)	11.4 sec.
Standing ¼ mile (400m)	14.1 sec.
Maximum speed	264km/h (164mph)

Cadillac ALLANTÉ

CADILLAC ALLANTÉ

Engine Capacity	4.1l (250cu in)
Weight	1585kg (3494lb)
Power	125kW (170bhp)
Torque	325.4Nm (240lb-ft) @ 2200 rpm
Price	$54,700
Acceleration:	
0–30mph (48km/h)	3.4 sec.
0–60mph (96km/h)	8.3 sec.
0–100mph (160km/h)	11.6 sec.
Standing ¼ mile (400m)	14.1 sec.
Maximum speed	265km/h (165mph)

A Cadillac like no other that had gone before it, or has followed since, the Allanté was the American manufacturer's first foray into the world of luxury roadsters, and it was quite a bumpy ride at that.

With its simple Pininfarina-styled bodywork and traditional American underpinnings, the Allanté is a strange fruit that set tongues wagging when it was new and continues to do the same today. People either loved or loathed it, but it was designed with two purposes in mind: firstly to restore some credibility to the marque, and secondly to compete head-on with cars like the Mercedes 560 SL.

One of the Allanté's major drawbacks was that it was the most expensive Cadillac thus far and cost only fractionally less than the popular and much better built SL. Customers opted for the status and stronger resale values of the Mercedes rather than take a gamble on the controversial Cadillac, so it's hardly surprising that it sold in limited numbers before Cadillac knocked it on the head.

As exotic and unusual as the Allanté is, it struggles to compete with the Mercedes when it comes to performance. It's only 11km/h (7mph) slower than the German roadster, but the Caddy feels more sluggish and less eager to respond when the two are tested back-to-back.

Mercedes-Benz 560 SL

Inside Story

Introduced in 1971, the W107 Mercedes SL was successful and long-lived. Like many European cars of the time, it has a unitary body and chassis, resulting in a very stiff structure. Suspension is all-independent, with upper and lower A-arms and coil springs at the front, plus semi-trailing arms at the rear, also coil-sprung. Self-levelling shock absorbers are standard to provide outstanding cornering ability. Four-wheel, anti-lock brakes are fitted to all 560 SLs.

POWER PACK

Conceived as the most powerful member of the R107/W116 family, the 560 SL introduced a new engine, the 5549cc (338cu in) M117 also found in the 1987 SE/SEL and SEC models. This all-alloy, linerless engine features a nearly square bore and stroke and a single camshaft for each bank, with two valves per cylinder. With 9.0:1 compression pistons and Bosch electronic fuel injection it was rated at 167kW (227bhp) in US trim with full emissions equipment.

Handling

It may be called an SL, but the Mercedes is a heavyweight. Nevertheless, it is easier to pilot through bends at high speed and exhibits less body roll.

Performance

With a bigger engine and a more intelligent, rear-drive chassis, the 560 SL would seem to be the winner on paper and indeed it is, but really not by that much. Its 0–96km/h (0–60mph) time is only 0.3 of a second quicker than the Allanté, but feels somewhat more.

Cadillac ALLANTÉ

Inside Story

It may look unique and glamorous, but beneath its sharply tailored suit the Allanté shares many parts with lesser Cadillacs. The basic floorpan was derived from the 1986 E-body Eldorado and sent to Turin in Italy where the bodywork was grafted on. The shells were then galvanized and sent back to Detroit where the running gear was attached. The Allanté boasts all-independent suspension courtesy of MacPherson struts. Anti-roll bars front and rear aid handling and there are four-wheel disk brakes.

POWER PACK

During the course of its lifetime, the Allanté got three different powerplants. Early cars (1987–88) were powered by a 4080cc (249cu in/4.1-liter) V8. This aluminum block engine with alloy heads was introduced in 1982 with standard digital fuel injection. On the Allanté, it was rated at 125kW (170bhp) versus 95kW (130bhp) on other models. This was mainly due to a tuned intake, less restrictive heads, Multi instead of dual-point fuel injection and roller rockers.

Ride

They both cater to a luxury-minded clientele, so the Mercedes and Cadillac both have a fairly soft, composed ride and even over many miles of freeway both cars are still agreeable to drive. With self-levelling shocks, the Mercedes has the edge when it comes to ride comfort, though the difference is barely noticeable.

Braking

Four-wheel disk brakes are fitted on both cars, but the SL requires less road to come to a complete halt. The Cadillac, considering its curb weight, does make a fine effort, however.

Chevrolet CORVETTE HARDTOP

Front-engined and rear-drive, with six-speeds, huge engines, vast power outputs and composite bodies with fixed roofs: the similarities between the Viper GTS and the Corvette hardtop are striking, but which one really comes out on top?

In the era of ever more complex supercars the Corvette and Viper are a refreshing nod to how things used to be before technology tamed fast cars. Both use sophisticated driver aids to function, but were built with traditional lightweight bodies, with massive engines powering the rear wheels.

The similarities between these cars are so striking that it's difficult to identify a clear-cut winner, so it comes down to examining the little details and comparing the costs. Obviously, the Corvette is the more wallet friendly at nearly $30,000 less than the $68,225 Dodge, yet the Viper

doesn't feel any more special for all that extra money. It might be the more exclusive vehicle but it's only marginally faster right across the range and acceleration is blisteringly quick in both cars anyway.

The Corvette has been in production in one form or another for half a century and is an all-American icon. The Viper is an incredibly potent machine but somehow it feels like a young upstart next to the car it so obviously draws inspiration from. In the final analysis, the Corvette is the easier car to live with and no one would think any less of you for going down the less expensive road.

CHEVROLET CORVETTE HARDTOP

Engine Capacity	5686cc (347cu in)
Weight	1438kg (3170lb)
Power	254kW (345bhp)
Torque	474.5Nm (350lb-ft) @ 4400 rpm
Price	$38,320
Acceleration:	
0–60mph (96km/h)	4.9 sec.
0–100mph (148km/h)	11.3 sec.
0–150mph (240km/h)	29.5 sec.
Standing ¼ mile (400m)	13.3 sec.
Maximum speed	270km/h (168mph)

Dodge VIPER GTS

DODGE VIPER GTS

Engine Capacity	7996cc (30cu in)
Weight	1533kg (3380lb)
Power	331kW (450bhp)
Torque	650Nm (480lb-ft) @ 3600 rpm
Price	$68,225
Acceleration:	
0–60mph (96km/h)	4.5 sec.
0–100mph (148km/h)	11.9 sec.
0–150mph (240km/h)	28.7 sec.
Standing ¼ mile (400m)	12.9 sec.
Maximum speed	277km/h (172mph)

The Viper GTS is the undisputed king of modern American muscle cars. It's also the most powerful Dodge ever produced and while the Corvette is probably the better choice for dedicated road use, the Viper is the more popular machine among both amateur and professional racing drivers. The GTS even has a distinctive "double-bubble" roof line to accommodate crash helmets, so is obviously the more dedicated track weapon.

Consequently, it doesn't really matter that the Corvette boasts a better equipped and more comfortable cabin or that it's the better daily driver. The Viper appeals to those looking for an extreme machine to have some serious track fun in. And few cars can match the Viper's charisma or macho appeal.

Nor can the Corvette match its performance. There might only be a tiny difference on the stopwatch, but the Dodge feels the edgier, more raw and involving machine. It's a staggering performer by any standards. Nearly twice the price of the Corvette, it still looks like a storming bargain compared to its European competitors.

Both cars have charisma and performance by the barrelful but the Dodge comes out on top simply because it feels more exotic and animal-like than the earth-bound Chevrolet.

Chevrolet CORVETTE HARDTOP

Inside Story

The Corvette recipe is one of the most famous in the world: a steel chassis clothed by a fiberglass body with the whole structure made incredibly stiff by a bonded composite/balsa-wood floor and hardtop. The suspension is a work of art, with sculpted alloy double wishbones at the front and a complex multilink system with toe control links at the rear. A rear-mounted transaxle helps the 'Vette achieve near-perfect weight distribution.

P O W E R   P A C K

Its spec makes it sound like an old V8 from years ago, with just two valves per cylinder, a single camshaft buried deep in the V8 and pushrods, rockers and hydraulic lifters. The difference is that its displacement is 5686cc (347cu in) and it has an alloy rather than a cast-iron block. With a 10.0:1 compression ratio, advanced engine management and electronic fuel injection, it pumps out a genuine 254kW (345bhp) and 474.5Nm (350lb-ft) of torque.

Ride

Although neither car is designed for maximum comfort, both having very stiff suspensions, they do surprisingly well, helped in each case by excellent seats. To really perform at their best, however, both need good road surfaces.

Accommodation

Early Viper interiors were cheap-looking, but the GTS is an enormous improvement. The fit and finish are better, the seats are supportive and the pedals adjust as a unit to give the perfect driving position. The Corvette is more stylized but is better equipped and feels more airy, with greater outward vision.

Dodge VIPER GTS

Inside Story

Like the Corvette, the Viper has a separate chassis, a composite fiberglass body and hardtop. Its chassis is composed of massive steel-box sections, making a perimeter frame. The bodywork is bonded on to form an immensely strong structure. As with the Corvette, it has double-wishbone suspension at the front and double wishbones and toe control links at the rear, plus rack-and-pinion steering and a sure-shifting, six-speed manual transmission.

POWER PACK

The Viper engine layout is traditional, with the cylinders in a 90-degree V and a single camshaft working two valves per cylinder with pushrods and hydraulic lifters. The difference between this engine and old V8s is twofold: the Viper boasts a V10 layout with six main bearings and is all alloy with removable cast-iron wet liners. The combination of sheer size 8000cc (488cu in) and sequential fuel injection gives it all the power and torque it needs.

Handling

It is more predictable than the original RT/10, but the GTS still feels more edgy than the Corvette and requires more effort from the driver. But it has slightly greater adhesion at the limit.

Performance

Drive the Corvette hardtop and you can't believe that there is anything significantly quicker, but then along comes the Viper. Although it has 73kW (100bhp) and 176Nm (130lb-ft) of torque more than the Corvette, this translates to a half second difference in the ¼-mile (400m) and not much more to 160km/h (100mph). The bottom line, however, is that the Viper is faster everywhere – through the gears, in each gear and at overall top speed.

Steeda MUSTANG GT

> The Mustang is America's pony car of choice, and also preferred among tuning companies. Two of the most noted are Kenny Brown and Steeda, which turn regular 'Stangs into supercar killers. But how do they compare?

Steeda has been synonymous with breathed-over Mustangs for over a decade now. So, if you want more kick from your pony car, it's a great name to call, especially if you don't have the budget for, or want to go as extreme as, the Kenny Brown route.

Steeda Mustangs are one of the more refined tuning packages available and, for the money, offer a lot of bang for your bucks. In fact, although it might be slightly slower to respond and accelerate than its rival, the Steeda 'Stang will continue onto a higher top speed, so in a marathon, rather than a sprint, it will emerge the victor.

More chuckable and punchy it might be, but the RS can't compete with the GT's superior stopping power. They've never been a strong point on any Mustang, but Steeda has addressed the situation better and its car will pull up sharper and with more reassurance.

Its built-in roll bar might make it safer for the track, but the RS is more cramped and harder to get into than the GT.

If you want the ultimate no-holds-barred Mustang and are prepared to pay for it, go visit Kenny Brown. But if value for money and usability are more important than sheer grunt, the Steeda 'Stang is the better choice.

STEEDA MUSTANG GT

Engine Capacity	4736cc (289cu in)
Weight	1506kg (3320lb)
Power	287kW (390bhp)
Torque	508.4Nm (375lb-ft) @ 4300 rpm
Price	$32,800

Acceleration:

0–30mph (48km/h)	2.8 sec.
0–60mph (96km/h)	5.4 sec.
0–100mph (160km/h)	12.2 sec.
Standing ¼ mile (400m)	13.5 sec
Maximum speed	269km/h (167mph)

Kenny Brown COBRA 289 RS

KENNY BROWN COBRA 289 RS

Engine Capacity	4605cc (281cu in)
Weight	1445kg (3185lb)
Power	353kW (480bhp)
Torque	630.5Nm (465lb-ft) @ 4450 rpm
Price	$ Not quoted
Acceleration:	
0–30mph (48km/h)	2.0 sec.
0–60mph (96km/h)	4.5 sec.
0–100mph (160km/h)	11.7 sec.
Standing ¼ mile (400m)	12.4 sec.
Maximum speed	265km/h (165mph)

There are some people in the world who always want a little more, be it food on their plate, money in the bank or performance from their car. Even when it's something as potent as the Mustang right out of the box.

So who would you trust to wring even more ponies from your pony car? Well, if money wasn't a deciding factor, the answer might be Kenny Brown and his Cobra 289 RS. This tweaked and tuned performer shows just how far you can go with the standard car and what the factory could have achieved if only it had the budget and nerve to take it all the way.

Both cars handle like thoroughbreds with their adjustable shocks and sportier suspension, but the RS shades it with its level 5 AGS suspension creating a snappier response and more neutral feel when traveling at the very limits of its ability. Of the two the Kenny Brown offering feels more like a racing car, and for that reason alone is the more exciting ride.

Its subtle looks give few clues to the phenomenal handling potential that lies beneath the surface. You cannot sniff at 353kW (480bhp), and a 0–160km/h (0–100mph) time of just 11.7 seconds makes this as close to a modern-day version of the Shelby GT-350R as they come.

Steeda MUSTANG GT

Inside Story

The Fox-platform Mustang has arguably become the most popular platform among the tuner contingent. From 1994 and onward, the Fox-4 platform cars have a stiffer structure, making them more suitable for performance applications. Turning a GT into a Steeda includes adding an Auburn locker differential with 3.73 gears, Steeda sport springs, five-way adjustable shocks, strut tower, G-Load braces, heavy-duty rear upper control arms, aluminum rear lower arms, offset bushings and upgraded Cobra disk brakes.

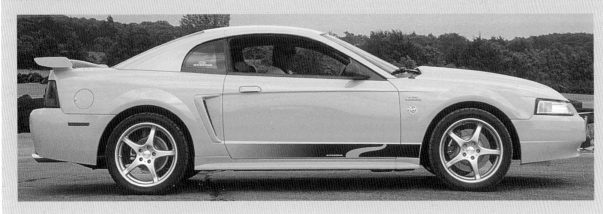

POWER PACK

When the 4.6 liter OHC-2V motor debuted late in 1995, tuners were worried that the onboard diagnostics would prevent radical modifications. This proved to be unfounded. Steeda fits a K&N filter-charger kit, a bigger 7cm (2.8in) throttle body, and stainless-steel 6cm (2.25in) Super Quiet mufflers to satisfy driveby noise standards. A super-charger kit enables this pony to crank out more than 279kW (380bhp), an increase over the stock 1999 Cobra.

Braking

In the past, the one weak link in the Mustang was its braking power. This has changed since the debut of the SN-95. Both of these cars go a great deal further, with big four-wheel disks and heavy-duty pads. The 289, with its huge Brembo front rotors and Kevlar pads, has a slight advantage when it comes to stopping, but the Steeda, with its 33cm (13in) front and 29cm (11.5in) rear disks, still stops far quicker and shorter than a comparable stock GT.

Road holding

Huge wheels and extra-sticky tires (Firestone SZ-50s on the 289 and 275/40/17s on the Steeda) translate into supercar levels of poise and grip. The 289 does, however, have a very slight edge.

Kenny Brown COBRA 289 RS

Inside Story

Riding on a heavily modified version of the original 1979 chassis, codenamed Fox-4, the 1997 Mustang employs unitary construction, modified MacPherson struts and a live rear axle. Modifications to the 289 RS include a Kenny Brown-enhanced suspension, with Bilstein struts and shocks with Sport springs, plus a Level 5 Advanced geometry system, with adjustable control arms and panhard rod at the rear. The four-wheel disk brakes incorporate Kevlar pads.

POWER PACK

This car started off life as a 1997 Mustang Cobra, which means a 4.6-liter quad cam, Romeo V8, with 224kW (305bhp). It has subsequently been stroked to 4736cc (289cu in), fitted with forged-alloy racing pistons, forged-steel rods, a high-volume oil pan with a full-length windage tray to improve oil control, ceramic-coated exhaust headers and a Vortech Supercharger with 62 kPa (9 psi) of boost. Fully balanced and blue-printed, it cranks out over 346kW (470bhp).

Accommodation

Mustangs have never been big on interior space, and this holds true for the SN-95 cars. The front buckets offer adequate support, but the rear seat is only for children. With a built-in roll bar, the 289 RS is harder to squeeze into, but the tradeoff is increased stiffness and safety.

Ride

Despite incredible handling, both cars ride much better than you would expect. The adjustable shocks and urethane bushings mean that they are surprisingly comfortable daily drivers.

Against the Clock

While it's all well and good comparing one legendary supercar rival against another legendary supercar rival, what about machines built by the same manufacturer, several years or decades apart? In this chapter we look at cars designed to replace previous models in our hearts and minds; vehicles like the new BMW M5, which we compare with its previous, identically-named incarnation?

Setting up comparisons in this way allows us to see just how far a particular carmaker has pushed itself and progressed over the years. For example, is Jaguar guilty of resting on its laurels since it came up with the XKE, or is the XJR a giant leap forward in both technology and handling for the big cat? Or is one Monte Carlo really worth trading in for another Monte Carlo?

Certainly, the cars chosen to go head to head in this chapter offer some of the most direct and quantifiable comparisons available, and this in itself makes for some truly fascinating reading.

However, there's more going on in this chapter than simple comparisons of pairs of cars from the same family. That would be far too easy. How does one car, obviously inspired by another from an earlier motoring era, fare against its inspiration, when the pair are driven side by side? Have advancements in technology enabled us to build better machinery, or did we get it right first time and lose the formula along the way? Hence the perhaps unlikely pairing of the awesome Mercedes 300SL Gullwing and the underdeveloped De Lorean. Like chalk and cheese to drive, both are exclusive and crammed full of character, and DeLorean made no bones about where it got the idea for the DMC's famous doors, so it's only right that it should stand up and be counted. Who said you can't teach an old dog new tricks?

Mercedes-Benz 300 SL

When John DeLorean wanted to make a sports car, part of his inspiration came from the immortal Mercedes 300 SL, from which he copied the gullwing doors. But 30 years later, was it as good as the Mercedes?

Two cars and two distinctive sets of gullwing doors, but while one was dubbed "the sports car of the future" by the American motoring press the other only got to play the part in the movies. And it was the German that occupied the role in the real world.

Developed from a Le Mans winning sports car, the Mercedes was the fastest road car in the world at its launch, whereas the DeLorean always lacked the pace its looks deserved. With its detuned Renault designed V6, the DeLorean struggles to exceed 160km/h (100mph), while the SL feels rapid even by today's standards. In fact, in factory tune it can rocket to 220km/h (135mph) and way beyond when

modified. More power would have made the DeLorean a bit more inspiring to drive, but the SL has so much it always entertains, and thanks to its rear twin-pivot swing axle, there is a constant supply of oversteer on tap should you want it.

More of a handful on the road and more of an eyeful when parked, the SL is often cited as being one of the most beautiful designs in automotive history. It is also possibly the only car as sexy with its doors open as when they're closed. Viewed alongside, its dowdy stainless-steel counterpart simply can't hold a candle to it.

MERCEDES-BENZ 300 SL

Engine Capacity	2996cc (183cu in)
Weight	1293kg (2850lb)
Power	176kW (240bhp)
Torque	292.9Nm (216lb-ft) @ 4800 rpm
Price	$7030
Acceleration:	
0–30mph (48km/h)	3.5 sec.
0–60mph (96km/h)	9.0 sec.
0–90mph (148km/h)	17.5 sec.
Standing ¼ mile (400m)	16.1 sec.
Maximum Speed	217km/h (135mph)

DeLorean DMC

DELOREAN DMC

Engine Capacity	2840cc (173cu in)
Weight	1290kg (2840lb)
Power	106kW (145bhp)
Torque	219.6Nm (162lb-ft) @ 2750 rpm
Price	$25,600
Acceleration:	
0–30mph (48km/h)	4.0 sec.
0–60mph (96km/h)	9.6 sec.
0–90mph (148km/h)	31.0 sec.
Standing ¼ mile (400m)	17.9 sec.
Maximum Speed	200km/h (125mph)

With a chassis designed by sports car handling gurus Lotus, the DeLorean should have been a great car, but as it was, only 8000 rolled out of the Northern Ireland factory before it could be developed further and the company folded.

While it might not be as rapid as the Mercedes, the DeLorean has time on its side and benefits from newer technology, so it can stop much faster when it needs to. Its reassuringly efficient disks are decades better than the antiquated drums on which the Mercedes relies and which are apt to fade.

However, the Lotus-engineered chassis makes the DeLorean the more forgiving and easy-going machine to drive. Boasting high levels of grip and impressive cornering ability, it has a tendency to understeer, whereas the SL is a real handful on the limit and can be dangerously unpredictable.

Both cars feature distinctive gullwing doors, but the DeLorean's were a style choice copied from the Mercedes, which were born out of necessity and always a compromise. The DeLorean is simple to enter and exit but it's a tricky process in the SL, with its high, wide sills and pivoting steering wheel. And, with windows that have to be removed, rather than wound down, it can be a stiflingly uncomfortable experience even just sitting in the Mercedes.

Mercedes-Benz 300 SL

Inside Story

A complex steel spaceframe (weighing only 80kg/179lb) under the steel and alloy body houses a front-mounted straight-six engine and four-speed transmission, with front double-wishbone suspension and simple swing axles and trailing arms at the rear. Gullwing doors are a necessity as the spaceframe chassis needs high side members to be strong enough, leaving no space for conventional doors. Braking is by large four-wheel finned drums.

P O W E R   P A C K

The 300 SL engine started as a cast-iron block overhead-cam six with just 84kW (115bhp). In the 300 SL it still has just a single overhead camshaft operating two valves per cylinder. The valves are large, though: 5cm (1.93in) for the intake and 4cm (1.65in) for the exhaust. Thanks to a high compression ratio and mechanical fuel injection, it produces 176kW (240bhp) at 6100 rpm and 292Nm (216lb-ft) of torque at 4800 rpm. The engine can rev safely to 6400 rpm.

Ride

Mercedes needed to make the ride firm to minimize rear suspension movement. However, it's not as comfortable as the DeLorean.

Performance

The 300 SL could be geared for 265km/h (165mph), but in normal road trim still sprints to 160km/h (100mph) in just 21 seconds. It's almost twice as quick as the heavy, underpowered DeLorean, which really needs twin turbochargers.

Inside Story

The Lotus influence shines through. There is an Esprit-inspired folded-steel sheet backbone chassis with the rear-mounted engine between the "Y" of the angled chassis legs. The fiberglass body is covered in non-structural stainless steel cladding for effect and not for any engineering reason. Its radiator is front-mounted to help the weight distribution and the rear wheels and tires are bigger to suit the rear weight bias. Double wishbone front suspension is complemented by semi-trailing arm rear set up.

POWER PACK

DeLorean uses the Renault/Volvo/Peugeot all-alloy 2.8-liter V6 with a single overhead cam per bank and two valves per cylinder. With the Bosch K-Jetronic fuel injection, European-spec cars produces 108kW (145bhp) – almost 75kW (100bhp) less than the Mercedes – but a slightly more impressive 219Nm (162lb-ft) of torque. DeLorean planned to fit the engine with two small Japanese IHI turbos, but went out of business before the plan surfaced.

Handling

At the limit, the 300 SL's tail slides out if you lift off or give it too much power in a corner. If the tail-heavy DeLorean had more power it might do the same, but it understeers safely.

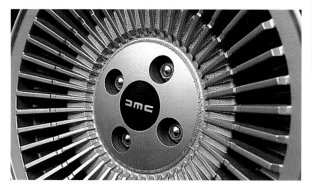

Braking

The DMC really excels in stopping as a modern sports car should. From 160km/h–0 (100mph–0), the DeLorean can be stopped in just under 46m (50 yards), impressive even today. The dated Mercedes still relies on fade-prone drum brakes.

Dodge VIPER

Separated by almost 30 years, the Viper and Cobra were created by enthusiasts. The cars follow exactly the same approach, putting the biggest engine possible in a lightweight car for uncompromising performance.

The influence of the Cobra is writ large all over the Viper, right down to the choice of name, but it's still very much its own animal.

Like the Cobra, the Viper has a massively powerful engine and simple chassis, but is a great deal heavier and more advanced. Car design has come a long way in 30 years, so it's hardly surprising that the Viper feels more refined. And the age difference is most noticeable on the road. The Viper is still tricky to control at speed, but displays no hidden vices so is the easier car to handle. Its more sophisticated suspension means it soaks up bumps and corners that throw the AC off line.

The Viper's huge ultra low-profile tires also provide better grip and road holding, even if they do communicate more bumps and thumps from the road surface to the driver – a plus or negative point, depending on your point of view.

Brake technology has come on over the last three decades, so it should come as no surprise to find the Viper has the better anchors. The Dodge's huge ventilated disks will bring it to a standstill from 160km/h (100mph) in 5 seconds, while the smaller, solid disks on the Cobra lock up when in a hurry.

DODGE VIPER

Engine Capacity	8000cc (488cu in)
Weight	1452kg (3202lb)
Power	305kW (415bhp)
Torque	610.1Nm (450lb-ft) @ 3200 rpm
Price	$64,000
Acceleration:	
0–30mph (48km/h)	1.6 sec.
0–60mph (96km/h)	4.7 sec.
0–100mph (160km/h)	9.3 sec.
Standing ¼ mile (400m)	13.2 sec.
Maximum Speed	260km/h (160mph)

AC COBRA

AC COBRA

Engine Capacity	7000cc (427cu in)
Weight	1150kg (2529lb)
Power	313kW (425bhp)
Torque	626.4Nm (462lb-ft) @ 2800 rpm
Price	$7495
Acceleration:	
0–30mph (48km/h)	1.8 sec.
0–60mph (96km/h)	4.6 sec.
0–100mph (160km/h)	8.7 sec.
Standing ¼ mile (400m)	12.4 sec.
Maximum Speed	265km/h (165mph)

A huge engine in the smallest possible package is always an intriguing idea. The result? Two cars, two snakes, both with a sting in the tail and enough performance to embarrass virtually anything else on the road.

However, the AC Cobra got there first. The brainchild of American racing driver Carol Shelby, the Cobra was one of the fastest production cars in the world at its launch, and although 30 years separate them, the AC still manages to be 8km/h (5mph) faster than the Dodge. This is purely because the smaller-engined Cobra has more power and less weight

to shift. And shift it does, as its better power to weight ratio gives it the faster 0–96km/h (0–60mph) time and a remarkable top speed of 265km/h (165mph).

But there's more to the Cobra than straight-line performance. As muscular and potent as the Dodge Viper is, it just doesn't have the looks or kudos of the legendary AC Cobra. Few cars are as revered or lusted after as an original Cobra; it's absolutely unmistakable from any angle and its curvaceous, open-topped body comes from a more stylish and romantic era, before wind-tunnels and committees brought their influence to bear on automotive design. What it lacks in refinement or creature comfort, the brutal Cobra more than makes up for with soul and passion.

Dodge VIPER

Inside Story

Like the Cobra, the Viper has a separate chassis but the tubular sheet-steel frame is stiffer, and has plastic inner body panels bonded on and an integral roll-over hoop to add to its strength. Double wishbone and coil spring suspension is used all around; there are massively wide rear tires; and the Borg Warner transmission is an incredibly highly-geared six-speed manual. There's power assistance for the rack-and-pinion steering.

POWER PACK

In the Dodge Ram truck the V10 engine is all iron. For the Viper it's all alloy but still has a single cam and pushrods operating two valves per cylinder. A displacement of 8000cc (488cu in) is plenty. The massive engine was partly developed by Lamborghini, then owned by Chrysler, and it uses electronic fuel injection with a sophisticated intake system. A dry-sump oiling system makes the engine low enough to fit under the Viper's hood.

Handling

Despite being difficult to drive at the limit, there are no hidden vices with the Viper. In total contrast, the Cobra can be incredibly hard work. It has to be wrestled through corners and is deflected by bumps the Viper shrugs off thanks to its sophisticated suspension.

Braking

There's less of the Cobra to stop but brakes have come on a long way since the early 1960s and the Viper's massive vented disks are grabbed by four-piston calipers at the front. They haul the Dodge to a standstill from 160km/h (100mph) in 5.0 seconds under perfect control, while the Cobra's smaller solid disks tend to lock up.

Inside Story

To suit the big 427 engines the Cobra chassis was re-engineered, with thicker-walled chassis tubes. A wishbone and coil spring suspension replace the antiquated transverse leaf spring setup from the AC Ace. The alloy bodywork had flared fenders to cover the big Halibrand alloy wheels. A Borg Warner four-speed is mated to the engine and four-wheel disk brakes haul the car down from more than 260km/h (160mph). These cars were so fast, the Shelby mechanics had a bet to see how long it would take one of these cars to return to the autoshop in a box.

Ford's big-block 7000cc (427cu in) V8 was a proven winner in NASCAR oval track racing. It was heavy, with cast-iron block and heads, but extremely tough with a forged-steel crank, very strong con rods and a generous lubrication system. The design was uncomplicated, with a single block-mounted camshaft operating two valves in each cylinder in wedge-shaped combustion chambers. Fuel was pumped in by two four-barrel Holleys.

Performance

The smaller-engined Cobra just has the legs of the mighty Viper, not because it's fractionally more powerful (which it is), or more aerodynamic (it isn't) but because it's a lot lighter and has a better power-to-weight ratio. On the road the Cobra's performance is simply more exhilarating.

Ride

The Viper's huge tires, which give it so much road holding, let it down when it comes to ride. They are ultra-low profile and transmit all the bumps and thumps from poor road surfaces. The older Cobra has much higher-profile tires. Despite its stiff springs it just has the edge over its modernday counterpart.

Alfa Romeo SPIDER

Italy has long been renowned as the home of fun-to-drive, sporty cars. Two of the current crop are the stylish Alfa Romeo Spider and the cute Fiat Barchetta, but which of these is the most rewarding to drive and own?

Think of a small, fun, and affordable Italian roadster and the car you invariably think of is the Alfa Romeo Spider. The Spider has been with us since 1966, but the contemporary version made its debut in 1994 and, bar the name, shares virtually nothing in common with its predecessor, the Duetto Spider.

Unlike the original Spider – although the same as the Barchetta – the new Spider is front-wheel drive and based on a modified Fiat chassis. Both cars are fun and frisky to drive but have their own unique character. The Alfa, for example, was significantly more expensive than the Fiat when new and you can both see and feel the difference when you jump from one to another,

with the Alfa having the more spacious and better-equipped cabin.

Both cars are lively performers, with the Alfa Romeo having more power to draw on and a slightly higher top speed. However, it's the Spider that feels the smoother machine when accelerating hard or over longer distances.

Critics may complain about the amount of chassis flex while cornering, but with careful inputs of throttle it's a trait that can actually improve grip and cornering speeds. But, should you get into trouble, the Alfa has the more efficient brakes and they're almost always enough to rein things back again.

ALFA ROMEO SPIDER

Engine Capacity	1970cc (120cu in)
Weight	1370kg (3021lb)
Power	110kW (150bhp)
Torque	185.7Nm (137lb-ft) @ 4000 rpm
Price	$36,700
Acceleration:	
0–30mph (48km/h)	3.3 sec.
0–60mph (96km/h)	8.9 sec.
0–100mph (160km/h)	29.2 sec.
Standing ¼ mile (400m)	17.3 sec.
Maximum Speed	210km/h (130mph)

Fiat BARCHETTA

FIAT BARCHETTA

Engine Capacity	1747cc (107cu in)
Weight	1056kg (2329lb)
Power	96kW (130bhp)
Torque	164.1Nm (121lb-ft) @ 4300 rpm
Price	$22,670
Acceleration:	
0–30mph (48km/h)	2.8 sec.
0–60mph (96km/h)	8.7 sec.
0–100mph (160km/h)	26.4 sec.
Standing ¼ mile (400m)	16.6 sec.
Maximum Speed	201km/h (125mph)

Fiat may have taken control of Alfa Romeo in the 1990s, but it didn't prevent them from building a fun, two-seater roadster of their own to draw sales away from the Spider. The little Fiat provides the most rewarding driving experience.

The Alfa is a rapid and capable car, but it doesn't possess the sharpness of feel that the Fiat does. The Barchetta feels more poised and eager to turn in for corners than the Spider, and there is none of the scuttle shake or chassis flexing that you get when traveling quickly in the smaller Italian.

Roadsters are synonymous with bone-jarring rides and unrefined damping. The Fiat comes out on top thanks to its suspension when traversing undulating surfaces.

Just 8km/h (5mph) separates the two, which is surprising because the Barchetta has the smaller-capacity engine and fewer brake horsepower. Perhaps even more surprisingly however, the little Fiat accelerates faster, feels more nimble and changes through the gears swifter than the Alfa Romeo does, so it proves the most fun to drive.

Both cars are guaranteed to put a smile on your face, but with its lower price tag, the Fiat will do it for less so represents better value for money.

163

Alfa Romeo SPIDER

Inside Story

Although the new Spider carries on the spirit and tradition of its predecessor, which was built until 1993, it is different in virtually every way. For a start, it is front-wheel drive and based on the shortened Fiat Tipo floorpan. Alfa Romeo developed its own all-new suspension with MacPherson struts and lower wishbones at the front and a multi-link set-up at the rear, all coil sprung. It is fitted with four-wheel disk brakes and has a five-speed manual transmission.

POWER PACK

The engine is the heart of any Alfa Romeo and the 2.0-liter four-cylinder unit in the Spider is a lesson in beautiful engineering. Its specification, including twin camshafts, twin balancer shafts, variable valve timing and four valves per cylinder, is straight out of the ideal book of engines and its power delivery, like that of many previous Alfa engines, is smooth and melodic. With 110kW (150bhp), it is also one of the most powerful normally aspirated 2.0-liter engines ever made.

Braking

Both cars have vented front disks and solid rears (in almost identical sizes), with the only real difference in specification being the Alfa's standard ABS. Both cars brake confidently, with smooth, consistent action and good pedal feel. Only under hard braking does the Alfa display its mettle, confidently out-braking the Fiat.

Accommodation

Both of these cars are easy to live with on a daily basis, being well laid out and reasonably spacious for two passengers. The larger Alfa has much better seats and is full of great design touches on a circular motif. The Fiat also boasts an excellent driving position and great design detailing, although the seats lack support.

Inside Story

Remarkably, the engineering origins of the striking Barchetta is based on the humble Punto – Fiat's small hatchback. Not much of the Punto remains, however, apart from the basic floorpan and the front-wheel drive layout. It has a MacPherson strut front suspension and trailing arms at the rear, with coil springs used all around. Like the Alfa, it has vented front and solid rear disk brakes, assisted rack-and-pinion steering and a standard five-speed manual transmission.

POWER PACK

A brand-new 1.8-liter four-cylinder engine was specially developed for the Barchetta. Typically Italian in character, it benefits from variable valve timing, 16 valves and hydraulic lifters. Its power output of 95kW (130bhp) is impressive for an engine of this size and 90 percent of its 164Nm (121lb-ft) of torque is delivered between 2000 and 6000 rpm. Although not as refined as some engines, it does have zing, very smooth power delivery and a raspy exhaust note to match.

Ride

Roadsters traditionally have bone-jarring rides and, by modern standards, these cars still do. The Fiat has the better damped suspension, but on undulating surfaces it becomes bouncy. The Alfa is even worse, crunching uncomfortably over bumps, with considerable chassis flex.

Road holding

Both cars grip extremely well around corners. The Fiat seems to cling to the road, however much power you apply. The Alfa's wider tires and brilliant multi-link suspension help it to really dig into bends, showing tremendous poise and grip.

Buick GS455

Buick muscle cars have always attracted a loyal following of enthusiasts who want both style and substance. But can the T-Type's turbocharged 3.8 liter V6 really give the big-block Gran Sport a run for its money?

C omparing any two cars is always a tricky undertaking, especially when one is a later reworking of a famous predecessor. But whatever gains are to be had in creature comfort and sophistication are invariably offset by a lessening of style and character. And so it is with these different generation Buicks.

The earlier GS began life back in the '60s as an answer to the Pontiac GTO and was steadily refined and improved until the GS455 emerged a few years later. Obviously a car as old as this will sport less sophisticated technology than the '80s T-Type, but it boasts something its successor lacks – classic style and soul. Often described as the greatest Buick of all time, the GS455 derived its name from its big-block V8

engine. Despite the age and technology gap, the earlier Buick has the larger capacity engine and generates so much power there is virtually nothing between them in terms of performance, although it's not as comfortable or refined as its younger brother.

Ultimately, the GS455 is the proper, real-deal muscle car, whilst the T-Type is the Johnny-come-lately that for all its obvious advancements lacks what it truly takes to steal the GS's thunder.

BUICK GS455

Engine Capacity	7456cc (455cu in)
Weight	1616kg (3562lb)
Power	257kW (350bhp)
Torque	691.5Nm (510lb-ft) @ 2800 rpm
Price	$3238
Acceleration:	
0–30mph (48km/h)	3.0 sec.
0–60mph (96km/h)	6.0 sec.
0–100mph (160km/h)	18.5 sec.
Standing ¼ mile (400m)	13.9 sec.
Maximum Speed	195km/h (120mph)

Buick T-TYPE

BUICK T-TYPE

Engine Capacity	3785cc (231ci)
Weight	1608kg (3545lb)
Power	173kW (235bhp)
Torque	447.4Nm (330lb-ft) @ 2400 rpm
Price	$13,714

Acceleration:	
0–30mph (48km/h)	2.8 sec.
0–60mph (96km/h)	6.2 sec.
0–100mph (160km/h)	10.2 sec.
Standing ¼ mile (400m)	13.8 sec.
Maximum Speed	205km/h (127mph)

Although the years may separate them, you can still see some strong family resemblances running through the Buick family. There can be little doubt that they were both shot from the barrel of the same gun. They share many visually similar styling cues, like front grilles, quad headlights, and full-width taillights, which over the years have become a recognized Buick hallmark.

Buick's designers haven't just rehashed what they already knew either. The later model now sports a more efficient and

lighter V6 engine, which has been turbocharged to provide the same sort of blistering performance its older brother produced the old-fashioned way, so it's the faster machine and will soldier on to a higher top speed.

You'll also find more modern, refined suspension technology helping the T-Type to negotiate corners. It will soak up bumps and imperfections in the road surface that the GS455 bumps and crashes over, and if only for day-to-day use and creature comfort, the newer car is the clear winner.

Buick GS455

Inside Story

Due to the massive big-block V8 causing a heavy front-weight bias, this A-body warrior is no corner carver. But because of the GS455's firmly planted coil-sprung four-link solid rear axle suspended from a separate steel frame, the power gets transferred to the 35cm (14in) tires via a Positraction rear with relative efficiency. Down the strip, this all-steel muscle machine packs a punch that knocked many a light out of the competition.

POWER PACK

Big, heavy and powerful with mega amounts of torque are the hallmarks of Buick's big-block V8. An oversquare design – with an 11cm (4.31in) bore and 12.5cm (3.9in) stroke – this cast-iron overhead-valve V8 displaces 7456cc (455cu in). A compression ratio of 10.5:1, big valves, a high-lift cam, hydraulic valve lifters and a large, single four-barrel Rochester carburetor mean it can generate 257kW (350bhp) at 4600 rpm and 691Nm (510lb-ft) of torque at 2800 rpm.

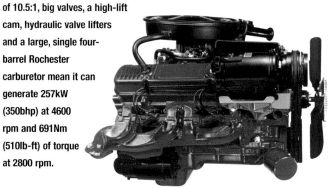

Road holding

Although the later GS has firmer shocks and springs and thicker anti-roll bars than earlier models, it can still be a handful through twisting turns at high speeds. The T-Type's stiff, separate frame and body construction, updated suspension design and modern lower profile radials are a massive improvement.

Accommodation

The basic, no-frills Gran Sport cabin provides a no-nonsense environment for the driver to concentrate his efforts on taming the 510lb-ft of torque. Optional digital gauges in the T-Type give it a futuristic attitude, while plush bucket seats pamper passengers like a Cadillac. On long journeys it is very comfortable and quiet.

Buick T-TYPE

Inside Story

Responsible for reviving the American performance muscle-car scene in the early 1980s, Buick's line of factory-tweaked G-bodies were king of both street and strip. The T-Type is basically a hot-rodded version of the standard Buick Regal and shares the G-body platform with the Chevrolet Monte Carlo and the Oldsmobile Cutlass Supreme. It is totally conventional with unitary construction, coil-sprung suspension and a live rear axle. By 1980s standards the brakes are antiquated with drums at the rear.

POWER PACK

Unlike its older brother, the GS455, the Buick T-Type relies on a more sophisticated form of power – a turbocharged 3.8-liter SFI fuel-injected engine. The engine has a 9.6cm (3.8in) bore x 9cm (3.4in) stroke, 8:1 compression pistons and sequential-port fuel injection. Each cylinder has its own coil pack and is controlled by an electronic fuel management program. The 3.8-liter engine makes a usable 447Nm (330lb-ft) of torque at 2400 rpm and 173kW (235bhp) at 4500 rpm.

Handling

A heavy-duty Muncie four-speed manual transmission and Positraction rear handles the 455's power with relative ease. To help lower rpm at highway speeds, the T-Type has a four-speed overdrive 200-4R auto transmission with 3.42 gears out back. Its tail can get loose during aggressive driving on wet surfaces, however.

Performance

Laden with huge amounts of torque, the GS's rip-roaring off-the-line acceleration spins the tires into smoke-shrouded oblivion, as opposed to the T-Type's smooth power curve that builds quickly as the turbo's boost rises. In the all-important ¼ mile (400m), the T-Type is quicker than the GS; in fact, it is quicker than most American cars of the 1980s.

Chevrolet MONTE CARLO SS 454

Primarily a luxury coupe, the Monte Carlo also spawned performance-bred SS versions in its early and later years. But does brute strength and big-block muscle really hold out over 1980s technology and sophistication?

Produced to compete in the gentlemen's performance-car market, perhaps the most accurate way to describe the Chevrolet Monte Carlo is as a steel fist wrapped in a velvet glove. Which is probably just as well, because the original muscle car era came to an abrupt end not long after the original hit the showrooms in 1970, and performance vehicles briefly fell from grace. Even so, the Monte was still a hit with buyers.

Both the original and later incarnations of the Monte Carlo are two-door, luxury coupes with room for four, but the earlier SS 454 is the bigger machine in almost every respect, and required the longest hood ever fitted to a Chevrolet in order to accommodate its gargantuan 7440cc (454cu in) V8 engine.

Almost 20 years separates the two machines, so there's no way you could reasonably expect the 70s Monte to handle as well as its late 1980s successor. However, it gives it a good run for its money. With so much weight over the front wheels the 454 understeers when pushed hard through the bends, but is the more capable car on the straights, where its bigger engine and greater torque give it the edge over the SS.

Overall, there's no substitute for engine capacity, and the more charismatic SS 454 is the one to go for.

CHEVROLET MONTE CARLO SS 454

Engine Capacity	7440cc (454cu in)
Weight	1570kg (3460lb)
Power	265kW (360bhp)
Torque	677.9Nm (500lb-ft) @ 3200 rpm
Price	$3123
Acceleration:	
0–30mph (48km/h)	2.8 sec.
0–60mph (96km/h)	7.1 sec.
0–100mph (160km/h)	15.4 sec.
Standing ¼ mile (400m)	14.1 sec.
Maximum Speed	212km/h (132mph)

Chevrolet MONTE CARLO SS

CHEVROLET MONTE CARLO SS

Engine Capacity	5000cc (305cu in)
Weight	1600kg (3526lb)
Power	140kW (190bhp)
Torque	325.4Nm (240lb-ft) @ 3200 rpm
Price	$14,838
Acceleration:	
0–30mph (48km/h)	3.1 sec.
0–60mph (96km/h)	8.2 sec.
0–100mph (160km/h)	16.2 sec.
Standing ¼ mile (400m)	14.1 sec.
Maximum Speed	209km/h (130mph)

Great movies always spawn sequels and so it is with cars too. Reworking the gentlemen's performance car for the 1980s led, not surprisingly, to the creation of the Monte Carlo SS, which might be less revered than its predecessor but is a better balanced and more usable all-round package.

Some things, however, never change, so the 1980s Monte also boasts a powerful, big-block engine under a mile-long hood, even if the wheel base is not as long as the 454's to handle it. But what it lacks in size and sheer grunt, the later car makes up for with better technology and handling.

Neither car corners very well – they just have too much weight and sheet-metal work to haul around – but the later Monte has stiffer suspension, better tires, and copes more admirably with sudden twists and turns.

Both machines are luxurious by muscle car standards inside, but again the later car is the more refined and easier to live with, even if does lack the charm and character of the earlier machine. Only produced in limited numbers, the SS might not be as desirable as the older SS 454, but it's an incredibly capable, rapid, and well respected muscle car.

Chevrolet MONTE CARLO SS 454

Inside Story

Introduced as a new model for 1970, beneath its formal roofline, the Monte was hardly new at all. Its G-body, 295cm (116in) wheelbase chassis was the same separate steel affair as used on the Chevelle sedan, and the wishbone front suspension and live rear-axle were standard in Chevrolets for the time. Coil springs in the front and rear give a smooth ride, though SS models received a stiffer suspension and standard front anti-roll bar.

POWER PACK

Chevrolet finally broke its 6555cc (400cu in) limit for intermediates in 1970, Listed on the Monte Carlo options list was the monster 7440 (454cu in) V8. A derivative of the 1965 396 Mark IV, it made plenty of power and had massive amounts of torque. The versions offered in the Monte Carlo SS were coded LS-5 and LS-6. The LS-5 made 265kW (360bhp), while the LS-6 made 331kW (450bhp). The latter was one of the most lethal engines available in 1970.

Braking

Although bigger in nearly every external dimension, the SS 454 is in fact slightly lighter than the Aerocoupe. When the central pedal is pressed, it seems easier to stop as well, although the front disks are more prone to locking up if care is not taken.

Performance

With nearly 2460cc (150cu in) more, the SS 454 simply leaves the Aerocoupe in the dust. Unburdened with emissions gear and fuel mileage requirements, it reaches 96km/h (60mph) more than a second quicker than the later Aerocoupe.

Chevrolet MONTE CARLO SS

Inside Story

Technology-wise, the downsized, 275cm (108.1in) wheelbase, third-generation Monte was not that far removed from the original. It retained body-on-the-frame construction and an independent short-long-arm front suspension, plus a live rear axle on semi-trailing arms and coil springs. The SS, reintroduced for 1983, used stiffer spring rates, revised shock valving and a bigger front anti-roll bar, plus a rear bar to improve cornering. Like the original, it retains front disc and rear drum brakes.

POWER PACK

After two oil crises, and with the onset of fuel economy standards and emissions requirements, the big-block was consigned to trucks by 1987. Thus the SS relies on small-block V8 power (in this case a 5000cc/305cu in engine). Still retaining two valves per cylinder and cast-iron block and heads, it features GM's command control computer, an electronically controlled Quadrajet carb and restrictive manifolds, but it still manages 140kW (190bhp) and 240lb-ft.

Handling

This is where technology really shines through. Though the early car does substantially well in view of its simple engineering, the Aerocoupe has better, more direct steering and feels more controllable. Goodyear Eagle tires give fine grip, though power-on oversteer is harder to attain.

Road holding

The 1980s marked a turning point in terms of handling for US-built cars. It is in this area where the Aerocoupe, with its slightly stiffer, radial-tuned suspension and superior tires, holds an edge over the big-block Monte. Although it weighs slightly less, acres of sheet metal make the SS 454 feel a tad more unwieldy, especially when confronted with a series of twisty back roads.

Plymouth PROWLER

Whichever way you look at it, the Plymouth Prowler is a head turner. But is it really worthy of being compared to the car from which it gets its inspiration, the legendary 1932 Ford Deuce Coupe?

Unashamedly retro, the Plymouth Prowler is a modern interpretation of the ever-popular all-American hot-rod. Looking like one of those concept cars all manufacturers wheel out to make their stands look more interesting at shows, the most unbelievable thing about the Prowler is that Plymouth actually built it.

It might resemble a traditional hot-rod on the surface but the Prowler is ultra-modern underneath, built as it is on an aluminum chassis and with many components adhesively bonded together. The Deuce Coupe by comparison uses a steel ladder-type frame and is screwed together like pretty much any traditional, backyard-built hot-rod.

Constructed from many modern components, the Prowler is obviously going to be the better car to drive – its more advanced engineering makes a huge difference. Using larger tires and the latest developments in suspension technology means the Plymouth goes where you point it with just a hint of body roll and understeer, even at high speed.

With the Prowler you get none of the hassle of an old car, so while the Deuce is still something of a compromise as old technology meets new to create a twitchy, demanding ride, the Plymouth has the kind of road manners that anyone can relax with and enjoy.

PLYMOUTH PROWLER

Engine Capacity	3523cc (215cu in)
Weight	1288kg (2840lb)
Power	186kW (253bhp)
Torque	345.7Nm (255lb-ft) @ 3950 rpm
Price	$40,000
Acceleration:	
0–30mph (48km/h)	1.8 sec.
0–60mph (96km/h)	6.0 sec.
0–100mph (160km/h)	20.2 sec.
Standing ¼ mile (400m)	14.1 sec
Maximum Speed	236km/h (147mph)

Ford DEUCE

FORD DEUCE

Engine Capacity	5817cc (355cu in)
Weight	1052kg (2320lb)
Power	309kW (420bhp)
Torque	596.6Nm (440lb-ft) @ 3,300rpm
Price	$490
Acceleration:	
0–30mph (48km/h)	1.7 sec.
0–60mph (96km/h)	4.2 sec.
0–100mph (160km/h)	12.9 sec.
Standing ¼ mile (400m)	14.1 sec.
Maximum Speed	201km/h (125mph)

The popularity of the '32 Ford three-window Coupe shows no signs of diminishing any time soon. Combining old-school looks with a small-block V8 gives the little Ford the go to match its show and while the Plymouth is a modern recreation, the Deuce is the real deal.

The car above might look like a '30s Ford on the outside, but the bodywork is actually fiberglass, and conceals more advanced and robust running gear in place of the ancient original equipment. In this way it has more in common with the Prowler than vintage Ford. Both cars look like refugees from the drag-strip but as quick as they are it is the Ford that would trip the timing lights first.

The Plymouth has more creature comforts to cope with modern driving demands, but the Deuce has more space once you're inside, better visibility and more supportive bucket seats. With its rear-hinged doors it's also easier to climb in and out of – but they are called 'suicide doors' for a reason.

Nostalgia is a wonderful thing but as good as it is, why not go the whole hog and do it properly? The Prowler is a brilliant reworking of a classic recipe, but the Deuce is the real deal and provides a full-fat hot-rod taste the Plymouth just cannot reproduce.

Plymouth PROWLER

Inside Story

Retro-looking it may be, but underneath the Prowler is very modern. It has a separate perimeter aluminum tube frame, with a composite and aluminum body. Most other components are from the parts bin. The Eagle Vision sedan donates the engine and transaxle; the latter is relocated from front to rear and requires a new driveshaft and new front cover. The suspension was borrowed from the Viper, and the steering is from a Plymouth Voyager.

POWER PACK

Prowlers can be divided into two distinct models – 1997 and 1999. The early cars are powered by a 3.5-liter, 157kW (214bhp), quad-cam V6, also used in the LH sedans. However, this proved only adequate, so for 1999, a much more powerful DOHC V6, packing 186kW (253bhp) and 345Nm (255lb-ft) of torque took its place. This all-aluminum alloy 24-valve engine with a distributor-less ignition system and sequential multiport fuel injection is the most powerful in its class.

Braking

Vented disks front and rear means the Prowler can go from 96km/h (60mph) to a standstill in 45m (148ft). The surprise is how amazingly close the Ford comes, its four-wheel disks enabling it to stop within a whisker of 46m (150ft).

Road holding

Sophisticated engineering pays off here. The Prowler, with its more advanced chassis, suspension and bigger tires, really has the edge over the Deuce and stays firmly planted to the road's surface. The Ford is not really at home on curvy or bumpy roads.

Inside Story

A basic shape is about all this Deuce shares with a stock 1932 Ford Model 18 coupe. It has fiberglass body panels, a custom-built steel ladder-type frame and, in place of the old beam axle and transverse leaf spring found on original stock roadsters, is a Ford 23cm (9in) live axle mounted with a four link and coil spring setup. At the front is a fully independent setup with upper and lower A-arms, plus coil-over spring/shock units and an anti-roll bar. Because it is capable of such incredible speeds, this particular Deuce has been fitted with four-wheel disk brakes sourced from GM Performance parts.

POWER PACK

Between the framerails of this nostalgic street rod lies the definitive powerplant: a 5735cc (350cu in) small-block Chevy V8. It has been over-bored by 0.762mm (0.030in) and fitted with a noticeably lopy Competition Cams 280 Magnum high-lift camshaft, cast-aluminum World Products Dart II Sportsman heads, and an Edelbrock aluminum intake manifold and a Performer 600-cfm four-barrel carburetor. The result is an incredible 309kW (420bhp).

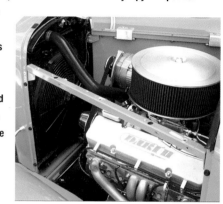

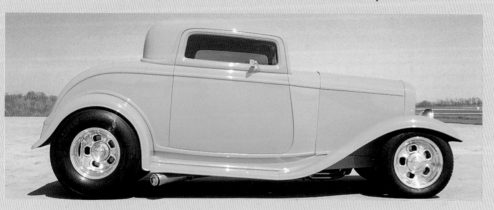

Ride

There really is little to choose between these two vehicles. Both deliver a fairly firm ride with less suspension travel than most passenger cars, but the Ford does a slightly better job at isolating its occupants.

Performance

Even though it offers enthusiastic low-end torque, the Prowler is more at home cruising the boulevard than engaging in stop-light drag races. The Deuce, with its small-block V8 and leaner demeanor, clearly has the edge. The lightweight coupe charges to 96km/h (60mph) in just over four seconds and can run the ¼-mile (400m) in the high 12-second range.

BMW M5 E28

BMW's Motorsport division has produced some fine cars, but perhaps none is more revered than its legendary "hot" 5-series cars. The original M5 was a scorcher in its day, but how does it measure up to its current namesake?

Grace, space, and plenty of pace would be the most concise way to sum up the BMW 5-Series experience. The Bavarian Motor Works has produced some of the best all-round executive saloons in recent years and the M5is the high-performance version everyone wants.

The first M5 broke cover at the Amsterdam Motor Show in 1984 and has been a staple ever since. Sticking to the same tried-and-tested formula over and over again has kept enthusiasts coming back for more of what they know. That way, they get a familiarly sporty and opulent car that handles as they'd expect it to, but has the latest looks to keep them one step ahead of the Joneses.

And the M5 was right from the start. The E28 version might be getting on in years, but it matches its modern replacement surprisingly closely. Both will exceed the 240km/h (150mph) mark and will do so with less fuss than their contemporaries. But, from 0–96km/h (0–60mph), the later car has the E28 beat, although it's still an incredibly rapid machine in its own right.

Time marches on and as good as the E28 is, it just isn't a patch on its worthy successor.

BMW M5 E28

Engine Capacity	3453cc (211cu in)
Weight	1551kg (3420lb)
Power	188kW (256bhp)
Torque	498.9Nm (368lb-ft) @ 3800 rpm
Price	$46,500
Acceleration:	
0–30mph (48km/h)	2.8 sec.
0–60mph (96km/h)	6.2 sec.
0–100mph (160km/h)	15.4 sec.
Standing ¼ mile (400m)	15.3 sec.
Maximum Speed	240km/h (150mph)

BMW M5 E39

BMW M5 E39

Engine Capacity	4941cc (302cu in)
Weight	1756kg (3872lb)
Power	294kW (400bhp)
Torque	329Nm (243lb-ft) @ 4500 rpm
Price	$69,000
Acceleration:	
0–30mph (48km/h)	2.3 sec.
0–60mph (96km/h)	5.3 sec.
0–100mph (160km/h)	12.7 sec.
Standing ¼ mile (400m)	14.1 sec.
Maximum Speed	260km/h (161mph)

Bigger, better, faster. Just a few of the words to summarize BMW's approach to improving its models. The great thing about the German manufacturer is that it's always looking for ways to better its cars, so if there's a flaw or area that doesn't quite come up to scratch, the next incarnation is almost guaranteed to have addressed it.

Supremely competent in every area imaginable the E39 version simply has to be the better car here. It benefits from every conceivable advancement in technology, so it goes, stops, corners, and feels better than its older namesake.

Everything the old M5 did, the new M5 does better. It turns in more crisply thanks to its advanced traction control, generates more power from its engine and if you were to crash these two cars into one another, the driver of the E39 would come off the better for it thanks to its more advanced safety systems and air-bags.

Drive an E28 and then immediately climb inside an E39 and you'll see just how far the M5 has come since its inception. With Porsche-baiting performance, Jaguar-like opulence and Japanese levels of reliability, it's quite possibly the best car in its class for the money.

BMW M5 E28

Inside Story

The E28 M5 was pure delight. This understated sedan was given the full treatment by BMW's Motorsport division. The sport suspension featured stiffer springs and Bilstein gas shocks, patented Track-Link rear suspension, reinforced brakes with larger calipers, specially designed ABS, wider tires, high-geared steering and a reinforced Getrag five-speed transmission. It was perhaps the ultimate driver's sedan when it burst on the scene.

P O W E R   P A C K

The M5 shared its engine with the M6 coupe. The only difference was that the straight-six engine had to be at a 30-degree angle to fit under the hood. The lineage of this engine dates back to the M1 mid-engined supercar, and features a light-alloy 24-valve head, twin overhead camshafts and central spark plugs. Displacing 3453cc (211cu in), it had 210kW (286bhp) in Europe. American versions, with emissions controls, managed rather less at 188kW (256bhp).

Performance

The 1988 E28 M5 feels very fast, even by the elevated standards of 21st century performance cars, and will reach a credible 240km/h (150mph). The new E39 M5 is the quicker car, but the margin of difference is not as big as you might think.

Handling

The original M5 is a paragon of what is great about M-badged BMWs. It is a no-compromise enthusiast's car that corners superbly – much better than the notorious tip-toe oversteering standard 5-Series. It is simply great fun and surprisingly good, even by today's standards. But it is eclipsed by the new M5, which ranks as one of the world's best handling and most composed automobiles.

Inside Story

BMW fans had been craving a Motorsport-tuned 5-Series for three years before the M5 satisfied expectations in glorious fashion. Based on the acclaimed E39 5-Series, it has a reinforced suspension, which is lowered by 15mm (.6in) at the front and 10mm (.4in) at the rear, along with stiffer springs and shocks. Driver aids include Dynamic Stability Control and a Sport mode that changes the throttle and steering settings. The six-speed transmission is beefed up to cope with the 294kW (400bhp) V8.

POWER PACK

The 5.0-liter V8 engine in the M5 is one of the world's greatest powerplants. It is heavily modified over the standard BMW V8, most notably gaining double VANOS variable valve timing. There are extra cooling passages in the heads and hydraulic lifters, plus an ingenious pumping system to keep oil flowing through the engine during extreme maneuvers. The maximum power output is an incredible 294kW (400bhp) and torque is no less impressive.

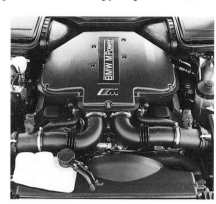

Braking

Back in 1987, the E28 M5's massively enhanced all-disk braking set-up and efficient ABS system were state of the art. Times have changed and the E39 car, with racing-style floating calipers and vented disks, can go from 0–96km/h (0–60mph) in just 2.8 seconds.

Ride

The Motorsport Division tunes its suspension for cornering ability rather than ride comfort. Both cars have a surprisingly supple ride quality, but the clear winner is the much more sophisticated new-shape M5.

Jaguar XKR

Jaguar has long been famous for its fantastic sports cars. Perhaps the most famous is the E-Type, and its modern counterpart is the supercharged XKR. Does it live up to the legend?

The XKR is the spiritual successor to the XKE and continues Jaguar's tradition of building rapid and refined luxury tourers. With looks that are a clear nod to its heritage, the XKR is the more advanced machine here and the years that separate them highlight just how far car design has progressed.

Compared to the XKE the XKR is a technical tour de force. Its supercharged engine is managed by sophisticated computer software to make it more efficient and provide optimum performance across the rev range, while the XKE relies on plugs, points, and traditional engine management. The XKR's impressive top speed is governed to 250km/h

(155mph) but with some careful tuning and remapping of its ECU can be made to go a lot quicker. By contrast, the XKE's engine technology was pretty much taken as far as it was feasible to go.

The XKR benefits from using the latest advancements in technology in other ways too. The newer model also has superior, low-profile tires, more efficient anti-lock brakes, and more highly advanced and better damped suspension. It will outhandle, outdrag, and outperform the XKE in every respect and is still comfortable and refined enough to use every day if you wish, which is possibly not something you would wish to do in its less sophisticated ancestor.

JAGUAR XKR

Engine Capacity	3996cc (244cu in)
Weight	1746kg (3850lb)
Power	272kW (370bhp)
Torque	524.7Nm (387lb-ft) @ 3600 rpm
Price	$107,200
Acceleration:	
0–30mph (48km/h)	2.3 sec.
0–60mph (96km/h)	5.2 sec.
0–100mph (160km/h)	12.6 sec.
Standing ¼ mile (400m)	13.7 sec.
Maximum Speed	250km/h (155mph)

Jaguar XKE

JAGUAR XKE

Engine Capacity	5343cc (326cu in)
Weight	1463kg (3225lb)
Power	200kW (272bhp)
Torque	412.2Nm (304lb-ft) @ 3600 rpm
Price	$8819
Acceleration:	
0–30mph (48km/h)	2.7 sec.
0–60mph (96km/h)	6.4 sec.
0–100mph (160km/h)	15.4 sec.
Standing ¼ mile (400m)	14.2 sec.
Maximum Speed	240km/h (149mph)

The XKE may be one of the last-of-the-line E-types and considered by many to be the ugly duckling of the family, but it's arguably still a prettier machine than the XKR. The E-type is a legend with an aura the XK can only dream of, and for all its on-board computers and cutting-edge technology, it will never have the charm, charisma, or following of its older brother.

Despite the gulf in years, the XKE is still only 10km/h (6mph) slower. Admittedly, it's not as quick off the mark, assured in corners, or comfortable, but it's still the more

desirable big cat. The later Jaguar might has a snugger-fitting hood and must-have trinkets, but what the E-type lacks in toys and creature comfort, it more than makes up for with soul. Its basic but sporty interior is more welcoming and is proof that you don't need half the equipment or extra weight modern sports cars like the XKR are burdened down with.

It might leave the XKE in its dust but the XKR will always remain in the shadow of its famous predecessor. From the era before driver's aids and computer-assisted designs, the XKE is more involving to drive, and in a world where looks are everything, it is still the looker of the family.

Jaguar XKR

Inside Story

Being a Jaguar, it has a traditional front-engine and rear-drive layout, with a V8 driving through a Mercedes five-speed automatic transmission. Double-wishbone suspension is on all four wheels, and its damping is adaptive to suit all speeds and conditions. Traction control keeps the power at an appropriate level, and ABS naturally helps the massive four-wheel disk-brake system. Luxury isn't stinted, though, so the XKR is a heavy 1750kg (3860lb).

POWER PACK

The V8 is made from aluminum alloy and has four overhead camshafts operating four valves per cylinder. The engine's dimensions are perfectly square with an 8.5cm (3.38in) bore and stroke; it revs happily past its 6000 rpm. High revs really aren't that necessary though, because Jaguar has added an Eaton supercharger to force-feed air into the combustion chambers. This raises torque to an outstanding 524Nm (387lb-ft) at 3600 rpm, giving the engine the pulling power of bigger engines.

Road holding

The enormously wide tires of the XKR give tremendous grip. The advanced suspension and precise steering make it feel much smaller than the E-Type. The E-Type has wide tires for its day, but they reach their limits much earlier.

Braking

The XKR, despite being considerably heavier, comes to a halt sooner from all speeds than the E-Type. The older car stands no chance against the ABS and vented disks of the XKR.

Jaguar XKE

Inside Story

The Series III uses the E-Type 2+2 wheelbase, which is 23cm (9in) longer than the standard two-seater E-Type. There were other modifications to the E-Type chassis to cope with the new engine. The E-Type structure consists of the central monocoque and a triangulated space frame that carries the engine and front suspension. The whole unit was generally stiffened and the track increased. The wishbones are inclined to give anti-dive geometry and the independent rear end uses longer drive shafts.

POWER PACK

The Series III E-Type was the first Jaguar to be fitted with the new aluminum-alloy, 60-degree V12 engine. Displacing 5,343cc (326cu in), it produced 200kW (272bhp) (184kW/250bhp in the US) and 412Nm (304lb-ft) of torque (strangled to 390Nm/288lb-ft in US imports.) The unit's two valves per cylinder are operated directly by a single, chain-driven, camshaft per cylinder bank. The Series III E-Type was the first British car to use a transistorized ignition.

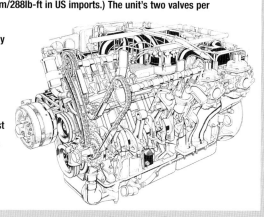

Ride

When it was launched, the E-Type, especially the Series III, was praised for its excellent ride. Even by today's standards it surprises – and it does so without all the electronic trickery of the XKR.

Accommodation

The XKR's interior has luxurious trimmings with a polished wood veneer dashboard and sumptuously stitched leather seats, but somehow it seems a little contrived. The E-Type is certainly more basic but is also much more sporty and classy at the same time.

Modern Warfare

If you are looking for proof of just how far car technology has advanced since a certain Karl Friedrich Benz (of Mercedes-Benz fame) made his first "Motorwagen" in 1885, then you need look no further than the machines going head to head in this chapter. It might be missing some of the more exotic and emotive cars found in previous chapters, but all of the machines on test here are fast, fun, and perhaps more importantly, affordable.

This means they're also more attainable to the average man on the street. For example, for less than half the price of a Lamborghini, you can get a good deal more than half the car by climbing behind the wheel of a Porsche Boxster or Mercedes SLK instead. Currently two of the finest roadsters available, is there really any reason to spend any more, when these cars do everything you could ever want, and more?

The machinery on display in this chapter represents some of the finest cars from all walks of life, be they rapid two seat roadsters, family sedans, top-spec boulevard cruisers, or hot rod inspired pick-up trucks. This chapter also does its bit for international cooperation, pitting American against European, and German against Japanese, to see once and for all who really does build the best cars in the world today. The results may or may not surprise you.

If the future of the muscle, sports, and luxury car is represented by this fine crop of contemporary offerings, things are certainly look quite promising on the hot car front. In terms of variety, affordability, and performance, we've probably never had it so good.

Cadillac DEVILLE CONCOURS

Bentley's Turbo R/T represents the ultimate in grand touring motoring. Cadillac's DeVille Concours is an attempt to build a world-class American-style tourer. But how does it measure up to Britain's best?

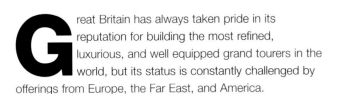

Great Britain has always taken pride in its reputation for building the most refined, luxurious, and well equipped grand tourers in the world, but its status is constantly challenged by offerings from Europe, the Far East, and America.

One such challenger is the Deville Concours. As the name implies, Cadillac's flagship model sets itself up to be the ultimate in refinement, and is a modern interpretation of luxury driving with a large twist of Americana thrown in.

Both cars are huge, luxo-barges, but whereas the Bentley originates from Europe and was designed to cope with its twists, turns, and winding side streets, the Cadillac was built to inhabit wide American boulevards. As a result it doesn't

need to corner so well, so has the softer springs and more supple ride of the two. With its electronic damping the Cadillac is one of the smoothest cars on the road.

Bigger than any other Cadillac that went before it, the Deville Concours is loaded with everything you could ever feasibly need; it's almost as quick to 96km/h (60mph) yet doesn't make such a huge fuss about it. If you fancy an impressive world-class tourer but want to be discreet about it, the Caddy is a sensible and vastly more affordable alternative.

CADILLAC DEVILLE CONCOURS

Engine Capacity	4.6l (281cu in)
Weight	1838kg (4052lb)
Power	220kW (300bhp)
Torque	412.2Nm (295lb-ft) @ 4400 rpm
Price	$46,900
Acceleration:	
0–30mph (48km/h)	3.1 sec.
0–60mph (96km/h)	6.9 sec.
0–100mph (160km/h)	21.5 sec.
Standing ¼ mile (400m)	15.1 sec.
Maximum Speed	210km/h (130mph)

Bentley TURBO R/T

BENTLEY TURBO R/T

Engine Capacity	6750cc (412cu in)
Weight	2476kg (5459lb)
Power	294kW (400bhp)
Torque	800Nm (590lb-ft) @ 2000 rpm
Price	$324,500
Acceleration:	
0–30mph (48km/h)	2.4 sec.
0–60mph (96km/h)	6.5 sec.
0–100mph (160km/h)	20.8 sec.
Standing ¼ mile (400m)	14.9 sec.
Maximum Speed	250km/h (155mph)

Bentley has always been the sporting counterpart to Rolls-Royce, but with its supercharged engine, tweaked suspension, and minor styling differences, this car has a distinct character all of its own.

The Bentley and its American rival boast huge proportions but the British offering is available in either short or long wheelbase versions, giving customers a better sense of choice. Whichever length they go for, either Bentley can out-handle the more ponderous Deville. Its stiffer suspension gives it a rawer edge and it feels the more sporting.

In terms of speed, the Bentley has a Garret turbocharger and more torque to get its bulky body moving, so will sprint to 96km/h (60mph) quicker and on to a higher top speed.

Elegant, comfortable, traditional and above all rapid, the Bentley Turbo will set you back $324,500 compared to the Cadillac's modest by comparison $46,900. Is it really worth so much more? Probably not, but emotionally it feels like it's worth every penny. The Bentley looks like it's worth a million, while the Cadillac is a bit drab and ordinary. If you could afford it, the chances are you'd go for the Bentley every time.

Cadillac DEVILLE CONCOURS

Inside Story

The DeVille Concours has its origins in the old 1986–1993 Sedan DeVille and it retains the unit construction chassis and a transverse-mounted V8 driving the front wheels. In 1994 the DeVille was drastically updated with an all-new body, revised chassis and suspension components. The Concours version benefits from stiffer spring rates and shock absorbers, plus higher performance Goodyear Eagle GA tires. Four-wheel disk brakes and ABS are standard.

POWER PACK

In 1993 Cadillac finally introduced an engine that made the European car manufacturers sit up and take notice. Known as the Northstar, this 32-valve, all-alloy unit is rated at 220kW (300bhp) and 412Nm (295lb-ft) of torque in the Concours. The block has a two-piece lower structure to quell vibration. The engine has platinum-tipped spark plugs which only need changing at 161,000km (100,000 miles), plus a special "limp-home" mode in case of coolant loss.

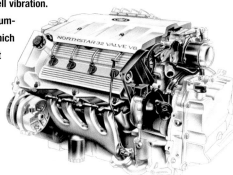

Braking

With its mighty 28cm (11in) vented disks front and rear, the Turbo R/T stops from a rocketing 96km/h (60mph) in 42m (139ft). The Concours also has vented disks front and rear and though it's lighter, it will brake from 96km/h (60mph) to a complete stop in 43m (142 feet) – just under 1m (3ft) shy of the Bentley.

Accommodation

Inside, the Caddy can accommodate six adults in comfort and offers substantial rear legroom. The Bentley is available in two different wheelbase lengths to suit the buyer and has a better interior fit and finish.

Bentley TURBO R/T

Inside Story

Turbo R/T is the name given to the fastest car yet made by the Rolls-Royce group – a model it called "the return of the silent sports car". The R signifies "road"-holding because suspension modifications have enhanced its cornering powers compared to the standard Brooklands model. Top speed is limited to 250km (155mph) in the interest of safety and because the stock tires cannot cope with the car's 2180kg (2.4 tons) at higher speeds. The vented disk brakes have standard ABS and two different wheelbases are offered, like rival luxury models such as the BMW 750.

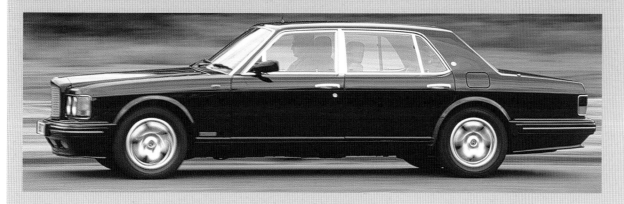

POWER PACK

The Bentley Turbo R/T is powered by a version of the standard Rolls-Royce 6.75-liter V8 in production since 1965. For 1998 the Turbo R/T received a liquid-cooled Garrett T04B turbocharger and air-to-air intercooler. This boosts power output from around 235kW (320bhp) to an impressive 294kW (400bhp). Despite the relatively low technology, it has Bosch electronic fuel injection and a Motronic engine management system.

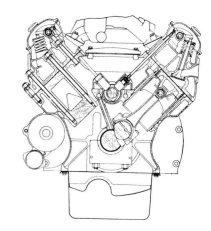

Road holding

Stiff suspension and bigger tires give both cars better grip than their lesser stablemates, but the Cadillac's lighter body weight over the obese Bentley gives it the edge.

Performance

The Bentley is only marginally quicker than the Cadillac, with 0–96km/h (0–60mph) taking 6.5 seconds compared to 6.9 seconds for the DeVille. The Cadillac's H-rated rubber results in its top speed being limited to 210km/h (130mph). The Turbo R/T, by contrast, will pull all the way past 240km/h (150mph).

Buick RIVIERA

One of the few big, traditional American coupes left, the Buick Riviera is also one of the most striking and best performing. But is it a worthy contender against the handsome Volvo C70?

Like the C70, America's answer to the Volvo is a good-looking car, but less showy than some of its flashy rivals, and you really have to look beneath the skin to fully appreciate its qualities.

As much as America loves the V8, in this instance you'll find a potent supercharged V6 in the homegrown Riviera. The Volvo meanwhile, "makes do" with a five-cylinder in-line motor that requires turbocharging to keep up with the Buick. Although this makes it the faster machine, the Swede performs best at high speeds when the turbocharger kicks in, while the Buick has more low-down torque and a more usable power band at legal speeds. On top of which, you

really need the manual transmission to wring the most from the Volvo's engine, and these have never been as popular an option in the US as automatics.

If you do most of your driving in Europe you'd probably go for the Volvo, but for the American motorist, the Buick might prove more comfortable. Not as sports orientated as the C70, the Riviera is set up for the wide open roads of North America, so has softer springs and a smoother ride.

The Volvo is the better driver's car, but the Buick is less expensive, more popular in the US and just as stylish.

BUICK RIVIERA

Engine Capacity	3785cc (231cu in)
Weight	1678kg (3699lb)
Power	176kW (240bhp)
Torque	379.6Nm (280lb-ft) @ 3600 rpm
Price	$32,500
Acceleration:	
0–30mph (48km/h)	2.4 sec.
0–60mph (96km/h)	6.9 sec.
0–100mph (160km/h)	15.2 sec.
Standing ¼ mile (400m)	15.3 sec.
Maximum Speed	222km/h (138mph)

Volto C70

VOLVO C70

Engine Capacity	2310cc (141cu in)
Weight	1526kg (3365lb)
Power	173kW (236bhp)
Torque	329.5Nm (243lb-ft) @ 2700 rpm
Price	$39,970

Acceleration:

0–30mph (48km/h)	2.8 sec.
0–60mph (96km/h)	6.4 sec.
0–100mph (160km/h)	15.1 sec.
Standing ¼ mile (400m)	14.9 sec.
Maximum Speed	250km/h (155mph)

Volvo of old had a reputation for building tough, reliable, and exceptionally long-lived but frankly uninspiring machinery. They were the kind of cars you could ferry a large family around in; safe in the knowledge it wasn't going to let you down and would hang tough in the event of an accident. But as reliability and safety became more of a given in new cars, Volvo lost its key marketing tool and had to change with the times. And the big Swede did this by coming back with a fresh new car complete with a sexy new image, so with the C70 Volvo's were suddenly considered cool.

Great looks and sporty handling now joined the accepted list of typical Volvo attributes and made the brand a credible alternative to the likes of Mercedes, BMW and in America, cars like the Buick Riviera.

It might look like an entirely new car, but beneath its incredible rigid body, the C70 relies on technology used in the old S70. Using proven technology and front-wheel drive has created a fine handling, sporty machine that will tackle twists and turns with more aplomb than the Buick.

With its super-charged engine, the European machine is also one of the fastest luxury coupes around, so can out-drag and out-brake the less nimble American.

Buick RIVIERA

Inside Story

Redesigned from the ground up for 1995, the Riviera uses the same front-drive chassis and suspension as the G-body Oldsmobile Aurora. This means unitary construction and an all-coil-sprung suspension, with MacPherson struts at the front and semi-trailing arms at the rear. The front bushings are soft to reduce harshness, while at the rear, aluminum control arms save weight and self-leveling shocks improve handling. Brakes are disks.

POWER PACK

Unlike the Aurora, which uses a 4.0-liter version of the Northstar V8, Rivieras rely on GM's 3800 90-degree supercharged V6. Displacing 3785cc (231cu in) and with 176kW (240bhp), it provides exceptional grunt, with maximum power coming in at 5200 rpm. The cast-iron pushrod engine also has a substantial amount of torque (379Nm/280lb-ft at 3600 rpm) – enough to rival some V8s. It is exceedingly smooth for a pushrod engine.

Performance

Both cars are similar when it comes to performance stakes. The Volvo is quicker to 96km/h (60mph), but the Riviera's greater torque means that it starts to catch up with its Swedish counterpart at higher speeds.

Accommodation

Although classed as a midsize, the C70 feels bigger than some rival coupes, though the Riviera makes better use of interior space and offers more supportive seats. The Volvo has an easier-to-read instrument panel, but the Buick's is more stylish and tasteful.

Volvo C70

Inside Story

Without doubt, the front-drive C70 is the slickest-looking Volvo in years, but beneath the sleek contours it is essentially an S70 (formerly 850) sedan. It boasts an all-coil suspension with front struts, and a semi-independent multi-link rear. Volvo has long used safety as one of the major selling points for its cars, and the C70 is no exception. Its incredibly stiff body has many safety features, such as SIPS (Side Impact Protection System) built into the floorpan, roof and doors. Like the Riviera, the Volvo boasts four-wheel disk brakes with standard ABS.

P O W E R   P A C K

Unlike the Buick, the Volvo C70 relies on a five-cylinder in-line engine. Of the two engines, the high-pressure turbocharged 2.3-liter unit is the most potent. Packing a credible 174kW (236bhp) and 329Nm (243lb-ft) of torque, it is potent and makes the C70 one of the quickest luxury coupes around. The engine is decidedly high-tech too, with an aluminum block and head, plus four valves per cylinder and dual overhead camshafts.

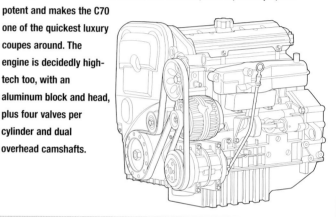

Braking

Both cars have four-wheel disks, but the Volvo's are larger, have bigger calipers and are vented in the front with solid rotors at the rear. Being lighter, the Swedish coupe is quicker to come to a rest from 96km/h (60mph), taking just 37m (123ft). The Buick is way behind, taking 42m (138ft).

Road holding

Slightly smaller than the Buick, the C70 also benefits from its firmer suspension and bigger rubber. It has noticeably better grip, and the 225/45 ZR17 tires give it more stability than the Riviera's higher profile Goodyears. On twisting roads, the Buick's larger size makes it feel a little more unwieldy, though its well-engineered suspension and stiff frame give it good poise. Fitting larger wheels and tires would make a noticeable improvement in grip.

BMW 540i

Ford's Taurus SHO has always been something of an enigma, yet it has the performance to challenge many European sport sedans. But does that include BMW's 540i?

At the high-end of the mid-sized luxury sedan market, the BMW 540i is a key player. More than that, it's one of the biggest fishes in a small and very exclusive pond, where its power and handling have won it as much praise as its refinement and build quality.

BMW's marketing men regularly describe their products as being the "ultimate driving machines" and although that's a pretty strong boast, it does hold water, especially when the 540i's competition is a Taurus SHO. The 540i simply feels the more complete vehicle and the performance figures certainly prove this to be the case, as the Bavarian will out-drag, out-

brake and out-corner its American competition. Few cars ride as well in this class as the BMW – the Taurus included. It was built to inhabit long, straight US highways, while the 540i was honed for the narrow, twisty roads and winding lanes of western Europe.

A true four-door, luxury road-rocket, the BMW can also boast better build quality, a more opulent interior and a more desirable badge than the Ford. It's hardly surprising it cost more to buy new and holds its value longer. If you want a rapid but refined autobahn stormer with plenty of snob appeal, it's really no contest. The BMW wins, hands down.

B M W 5 4 0 I

Engine Capacity	4398cc (268cu in
Weight	1680kg (3704lb
Power	207kW (282bhp
Torque	420.3Nm (310lb-ft) @ 3900 rpm
Price	$49,00(

Acceleration:

0–30mph (48km/h)	3.0 sec
0–60mph (96km/h)	6.2 sec
0–100mph (160km/h)	16.0 sec
Standing ¼ mile (400m)	14.1 sec
Maximum Speed	210km/h (130mph

Ford TAURUS SHO

FORD TAURUS SHO

Engine Capacity	3392cc (207cu in)
Weight	1540kg (3395lb)
Power	173kW (235bhp)
Torque	311.8Nm (230lb-ft) @ 4800 rpm
Price	$25,930
Acceleration:	
0–30mph (48km/h)	3.6 sec.
0–60mph (96km/h)	7.4 sec.
0–100mph (160km/h)	20.9 sec.
Standing ¼ mile (400m)	20.9 sec.
Maximum Speed	225km/h (140mph)

While it might not be the first car that springs to mind for Europeans when choosing a sporty executive sedan, the Ford Taurus SHO is a credible, capable and well known alternative to the BMW in the American car market.

For anyone unfamiliar with these Fords, SHO is an abbreviation of Super-High Output and is a reference to its all-alloy, Yamaha sourced V8 power plant. This engine is capable of propelling the Taurus to such speeds that in reality it is not very far behind the very capable BMW in terms of

acceleration, and even manages to better it with a higher top speed.

Both interiors come fully loaded, with the gadgets and gimmicks you'd expect to find in cars at this end of the spectrum. But, while the BMW is all sharp, angular lines, restrained hues and dark leather, the Taurus feels friendlier and less austere, with more generous amounts of head and leg room in the back.

With its boastful name and tailored styling, the Super-High Output Taurus is as brash as the BMW is understated. The Ford is a good car, but it is not the ultimate driving machine, even if it is more fun on the inside.

BMW 540i

Inside Story

The 540i is a traditional BMW design, with a front-mounted engine and rear-wheel drive. Due to constant refinements, it now has an incredibly stiff structure, despite its four doors, due to the increased use of high-tensile steel which comprises 40 percent of the bodyshell. The suspension has changed, with alloy control arms, hub carriers and brake calipers. In the Sport version, drive to the rear goes through a six-speed manual.

POWER PACK

To increase its US appeal, the 540i is powered by a V8 engine. Despite the 540i name, it displaces 4.4 liters compared to the original 4.0 liters. With a stroke lengthened by a fraction, its torque output is now a crushing 420Nm (310lb-ft) at 3900 rpm. The extremely sophisticated design includes four chain-driven camshafts with variable valve timing to give the best blend of torque at low rpm and power at high rpm.

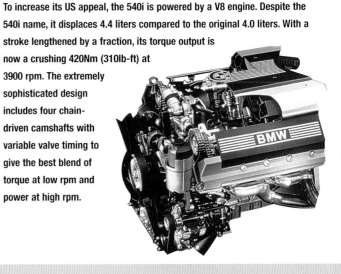

Handling

Both cars offer exceptional grip and the Taurus, with its active suspension, is surprisingly agile and comes out on top here. The Taurus has .80gs of lateral acceleration whereas the 540i has a .78g.

Accommodation

Inside, the cars are very different. The Ford is full of organic curves. The BMW is much more traditional and feels less gimmicky, despite the fact that both are fully loaded. The Taurus also boasts greater rear head and leg room.

Ford TAURUS SHO

Inside Story

It may be front-wheel drive, but the latest SHO has all the ingredients needed for BMW battling. It has rack-and-pinion steering and a more advanced suspension system than the BMW, with MacPherson struts at the front and a sophisticated quadralink system and active shock absorbers at the rear which alter the level of damping according to parameters like road surface and speed. The only transmission available is a four-speed automatic with a tall fourth gear.

P O W E R   P A C K

The Taurus all-alloy V8 has a much smaller displacement of just 3.4 liters compared to the BMW's 4.4. With a 173kW (235bhp) output, it actually produces more power per liter than the BMW (51kW/69bhp per liter compared to 48/65 bhp per liter).

Despite this, it cannot match the BMW's V8 for torque and needs to be revved much higher to fully exploit all of its power. Above 3000 rpm, eight secondary ports open to improve breathing at high rpm.

Ride

Nothing rides like a BMW 5 series, although the reactive shocks on the Taurus gives a smooth ride despite its handling prowess. The 540i is more at home on a twisty two-laner than on bumpy roads.

Performance

The SHO gives too much away. It has 37kW (51bhp) less power and its smaller engine just doesn't have the same low-down torque as the 540i. It also has to be driven much harder, and the taller gearing doesn't help either. Figures like a 15.6-second standing ¼ mile (400m) and a 225km/h (140mph) top speed are impressive, but the BMW is quicker still, reaching 0–96km/h (0-60mph) in 6.2 seconds and cruising comfortably at 210km/h (130mph).

Lexus LS400

The Lexus LS400 and BMW 740i represent the ultimate in four-door sedan refinement in the late 1990s. Swift and subtly styled, these flagship sedans are equipped with every luxury garnishing imaginable.

The Japanese have made an art of taking an existing product or design, ironing out any flaws or weaknesses, and creating their own, improved version. The Lexus is a perfect example of this strategy, and the LS range became the brand's flagship model, intended to take on and beat its established European rivals. In fact, it was specifically designed to tackle the likes of BMW head-on. The LS400 is certainly up to the challenge.

Like the 740i it handles better than a car as large and opulent as this should. Both are limited to an impressive 250km/h (155mph) top speed, but the Lexus will sprint from 0–96km/h (0–60mph) quicker – and do it quieter – than the

German. The BMW has the raspier engine note and feels more sports orientated, while the Lexus feels like it was designed to be luxurious first and to perform second. This shines through under normal driving conditions – which is what these machines are more commonly used for. The Lexus has the more refined low-speed ride and the sense of being shut off from the outside world in its more spacious cabin is almost uncanny.

If the Lexus has one major drawback it's that it doesn't have the badge appeal of the BMW. Good as it is, most car enthusiasts will prefer the more expensive 740i.

LEXUS LS400

Engine Capacity	3969cc (242cu in)
Weight	1762kg (3886lb)
Power	213kW (290bhp)
Torque	406.7Nm (300lb-ft) @ 4000 rpm
Price	$52,900
Acceleration:	
0–30mph (48km/h)	2.8 sec.
0–60mph (96km/h)	6.3 sec.
0–100mph (160km/h)	17.2 sec.
Standing ¼ mile (400m)	16.4 sec.
Maximum Speed	250km/h (155mph)

BMW 740i

BMW 740I

Engine Capacity	4398cc (268cu in)
Weight	1785kg (3937lb)
Power	207kW (282bhp)
Torque	420.3Nm (310lb-ft) @ 3900 rpm
Price	$59,900

Acceleration:

0–30mph (48km/h)	3.2 sec.
0–60mph (96km/h)	7.6 sec.
0–100mph (160km/h)	18.0 sec.
Standing ¼ mile (400m)	16.7 sec.
Maximum Speed	250km/h (155mph)

If, as BMW claims, it really does make the "ultimate driving machine", the 7 Series is arguably its definitive luxury sedan. It's fast, goes round corners like a car half its size and is as luxurious and refined as any of the competition, making the 7 Series the Bavarian Motor Works' most complete luxury car to date.

Built to draw sales away from its most bitter European rivals like Mercedes and Jaguar, the BMW 7 Series sets the benchmark against which all other top executive sedans are judged, and as undeniably good as the Lexus is, it simply doesn't have the kudos or snob appeal of the big German.

Classier on the outside and more opulent in, both cars pamper their occupants, but the 740i has the higher level of comfort, a much greater sense of character and just feels more special.

Neither car makes a song and dance about its capabilities but the BMW has the greater air of sophistication and although it's not as refined as the Lexus under everyday conditions, it has a definite edge when driven at speed. In fact, the BMW is one of the finest-handling machines in its class, as well as being one of the most forgiving. Amateur drivers will reach the limits of their ability long before the brilliant and ultimately more rewarding BMW.

Lexus LS400

Inside Story

There is nothing technically radical about the Lexus. Instead, Toyota engineers have paid incredible attention to detail to produce one of the most refined cars in the world. The LS400's handling and ride characteristics are unrivalled by its competitors. The seats have their own suspension system that allows the base of the seat to ride up and down. However, its only drawback is that the body on the second-generation LS400 looks too much like the first-generation's design.

POWER PACK

A light-alloy 32-valve 3969cc (242cu in) V8, noted for its smoothness and punch, has always powered the LS400. Variable valve-timing, lighter pistons and reduced friction push up the output of the 1997 LS400 from 191 to 213kW (260 to 290bhp). Power per liter is the best in its class and drive goes through a five-speed automatic transmission, which has crisper shifts than the old four-speed unit. The result is noticeable in the LS400's performance, producing a higher top speed and faster acceleration.

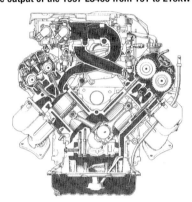

Performance

Through the gears these cars are very closely matched, as might be expected given such similar power outputs. The LS400 just nudges ahead however, beating the 740i by more than a second to 96km/h (60mph). Both engines are sweet, but the BMW's is a little more vocal than that of the LS400, a clue to its more sporty character.

Ride

As you'd expect, both cars excel in this department, but the Lexus set the benchmark for ride quality when it was first launched in 1990. It can still outclass the BMW, particularly at lower speeds where the feeling of isolation from the outside world is almost uncanny.

Inside Story

Although it looks very much like its predecessor, the 7 Series of 1994 is, for all intents and purposes, a new car. It is both longer and wider than before and has new multi-link rear suspension consisting of four transverse and longitudinal links connecting the wheel carrier to the subframe. There are struts and coil springs at the front, four-wheel disk brakes with standard anti-lock and a fantastic list of standard features that include a heated steering wheel and cruise control.

POWER PACK

BMW's V8s began to replace the venerable straight-six engines in the previous generation of 7 Series models as well as the mid-range 5 Series and the big 8 Series coupe in 1992. With four camshafts and 32 valves, this isn't only a potent and sweet-sounding engine but also a surprisingly thrifty one, delivering up to 11km per liter (25mpg). Power goes to the rear wheels through a five-speed automatic – another carryover from the old model.

Handling

Only here does the BMW begin to nudge ahead. It feels more fluent and agile than the Lexus, which on tighter corners and dips begins to feel its weight and size. Not that the BMW is perfect: its Servotronic steering lacks feedback and it doesn't have the turn-in sharpness of other upmarket German sports sedans.

Road holding

Through corners the grip of these big sedans is remarkable, and with the traction control switched on it proves hard to break the traction of the rear tires in either car.

Chevrolet 454 SS

In the early 1990s a select breed of performance trucks became an alternative form of sports car. Ford went for a more thorough design from its Special Vehicle Team, while Chevrolet relied on a huge engine and fewer changes.

There's no such thing as too much choice in this world, so it stands to reason there would be more than one performance-orientated pick-up truck to blow a little over $20,000 on. And you undoubtedly get an awful lot of truck for your buck in the form of the Chevy 454 SS. Take one for a spin and you're immediately conscious of how much sheet metal you're hauling around, even before you fill its capacious load bed.

Push it hard into corners and like the Ford it will understeer horribly until you bury the throttle and flick the tail round. The Chevy's enormous 7440cc (454cu in) V8 gives it more torque, brake horsepower and rapid acceleration than its counterpart, although both top out at 195km/h (120mph).

While it's true you could use either truck for hauling spare parts, furniture or anything else around with you, they're more like lifestyle accessories than workhorses, so how they ride isn't really so important. Neither handles particularly well, but the 454 has stiffer suspension and will corner surprisingly well and better than the big Ford.

Both are rapid and impressive-looking machines, but while the Ford is possibly the more accomplished all-round vehicle, personal preference will most likely be the deciding factor.

CHEVROLET 454 SS

Engine Capacity	5752cc (351cu in)
Weight	1986kg (4378lb)
Power	176kW (240bhp)
Torque	549Nm (405lb-ft) @ 2400 rpm
Price	$21,835
Acceleration:	
0–60mph (96km/h)	7.2 sec.
0–90mph (148km/h)	16.4 sec.
0–100mph (160km/h)	22.8 sec.
Standing ¼ mile (400m)	15.8 sec.
Maximum Speed	190km/h (120mph)

Ford F-150 LIGHTNING

Obviously, these are no ordinary workmen's tools. They're performance orientated showpieces, although the Ford has the better ride, with its softer sprung suspension, especially over rougher surfaces.

FORD F-150 LIGHTNING

Engine Capacity	7440cc (454cu in)
Weight	2057kg (4535lb)
Power	187kW (255bhp)
Torque	461Nm (340lb-ft) @ 3200 rpm
Price	$19,523

Acceleration:

0–60mph (96km/h)	7.5 sec.
0–90mph (148km/h)	17.3 sec.
0–100mph (160km/h)	25.9 sec.
Standing ¼ mile (400m)	15.7 sec.
Maximum Speed	190km/h (120mph)

If there's one vehicle America loves more than the muscle car it's the pick-up truck. Ignore the practical reasons for a moment and the most likely explanation for this is the sheer romance of them. They have a rugged, macho, go-anywhere, do-anything appeal that calls to mind the old pioneer/cowboy spirit and makes them the country's best-selling automobile.

The more rugged they are, the better; and there are few as rough and tough as these. Obviously, the Lightning wins the first battle by having the more testosterone-fuelled name, and currently outsells the Chevrolet.

You wouldn't expect something originally designed to work for a living to be as comfortable inside as either of these, but with bucket seats, plush carpets and elevated driving position they're relaxed and secure places to while away the hours, although the more car-like Lightning is the comfier of the two, so will leave you feeling fresher at the end of a journey.

One of the fastest trucks in the world, the only downside to driving the Lightning is how much you have to pay for the experience.

Chevrolet 454 SS

Inside Story

It may be a stunning performer but it's still a truck. The Lightning, therefore, keeps the same swing-axle front suspension with leading links and coil springs, while at the rear there is a live axle with leaf springs and an anti-roll bar. The difference is in the lower ride height, the stiffer springs, the uprated Monroe shocks, bigger anti-roll bars and a limited-slip differential. When that's added to taller 43cm (17in) wheels with Firestone Firehawk tires, it's a transformation.

POWER PACK

Ford's Special Vehicle Team took the familiar 5.8-liter Windsor cast-iron pushrod V8, with its two valves per cylinder, and worked their magic on it. Larger intake and exhaust valves are fitted inside recontoured combustion chambers and the ports are opened to let the engine breathe better. This is helped by revised intake and exhaust manifolds, with the exhaust leading to a free-flowing dual exhaust system. The engine also benefits from a revised camshaft for sharper response.

Braking

Both trucks have vented front disks and standard rear drums, and both have anti-lock brakes. The Ford is better balanced with a more reassuring feel to the brake pedal and, more importantly, it stops quicker and is less prone to locking up.

Ride

Stiffening up the suspension so much takes its toll on ride comfort. On smooth roads both trucks are fine, but at speed on a rough surface you'll pay for it, particularly in the SS.

Ford F-150 LIGHTNING

Inside Story

Chevrolet started with a theoretical advantage; its truck has a more car-like wishbone front suspension, although there is still just the usual truck live axle on leaf springs at the rear. The way forward was to stiffen it all up, with the ZQ8 handling package that includes higher-rate springs coupled with superior Bilstein shocks and a quicker steering ratio to let the driver stay in complete control. The easiest change was to the wheels and tires; large BFGoodrich Comp T/As were added.

P O W E R   P A C K

The Chevrolet's power comes from sheer size. With a fuel-injected, 7.4-liter engine not much tuning is required. The engine is the usual all-iron pushrod V8 design, with a single-mounted camshaft with two valves per cylinder. The little tuning that was done was to make the exhaust less restrictive. No attempt was made to make it a high-revving engine; all its power is produced by 4000 rpm and its staggering torque output of 549Nm (405lb-ft) comes at just 2400 rpm.

Accommodation

Both the F-150 and 454 SS have bucket seats and a commanding driving position. The quality and design of the instrumentation in the F-150 creates a more car-like interior.

Road holding

Both grip well but, not surprisingly, the taller and heavier 454 SS just cannot generate the same level of outright grip as the Ford, even though it's putting more rubber on the road with its 275/60s compared with the Lightning's 235/60s. The difference lies partly in the two trucks' weight distribution. The huge 7.4-liter engine gives a 59:41 front/rear distribution and ultimately that takes its toll.

Pontiac BONNEVILLE SSEI

Paying homage to the legendary Chrysler letter-series cars, the 300M boasts exotic styling, a roomy interior, and the most powerful V6 in its class. Is this enough to take on the likes of seasoned sports sedans like the Pontiac Bonneville?

I t might look like a regular family sedan but the name Bonneville implies land-speed records, blistering acceleration and all manner of excitement you'd normally associate with the famous Utah salt flats. And amazingly, for such an inauspicious looking machine, that's exactly what it delivers. Obviously you're not going to be breaking any records, and the SSEi may be getting on in years, but it still feels like a muscle car and handles better than its looks would suggest.

Like the vast majority of true muscle cars, the Bonneville is at its best traveling in a straight line and with the accelerator pedal hard to the floor. Against the clock it's faster all the way

to 160km/h (100mph) than the Chrysler and will leave it behind when both reach their top speed – the SSEi will do 222km/h (138mph) while the 300m can reach just 190km/h (118mph). And that's despite having less power than the Chrysler.

The Pontiac is better inside too, because what it gives away in interior space, it compensates for with better seats, a more comfortable driving position and a higher level of equipment. With its wide 60-series tires and firm suspension settings, the Bonneville is pretty competent in the corners, but its speed and creature comfort win it the most friends and make it the better all-rounder for everyday use.

PONTIAC BONNEVILLE SSEI

Engine Capacity	3791cc (231cu in)
Weight	1563kg (3446lb)
Power	176kW (240bhp)
Torque	379.6Nm (280lb-ft) @ 3200 rpm
Price	$28,425
Acceleration:	
0–30mph (48km/h)	2.2 sec.
0–60mph (96km/h)	6.9 sec.
0–100mph (160km/h)	15.0 sec.
Standing ¼ mile (400m)	15.2 sec.
Maximum Speed	222km/h (138mph)

Chrysler 300M

CHRYSLER 300M

Engine Capacity	3518cc (214cu in)
Weight	1615kg (3560lb)
Power	186kW (253bhp)
Torque	345.7Nm (255lb-ft) @ 3950 rpm
Price	$29,500
Acceleration:	
0–30mph (48km/h)	2.9 sec.
0–60mph (96km/h)	7.7 sec.
0–100mph (160km/h)	16.7 sec.
Standing ¼ mile (400m)	15.8 sec.
Maximum Speed	190km/h (118mph)

The flagship of the LH series Chrysler sedans, the 300M was built to exhibit the sportier side of its nature, and like the Bonneville is something of a wolf in sheep's clothing.

While it's undoubtedly slower than the SSEi, the 300M really proves its metal in corners and when the going gets rough. Fitted with special handling suspension, it boasts outstanding levels of grip, and will cling on when the Pontiac gives up and lets go. Because it's set up with handling rather than comfort in mind, the 300M isn't as smooth under normal conditions but feels more alive and interesting to drive than the Chrysler.

Should you get too carried away and things get out of shape, it's reassuring to know that the Chrysler will pull up shorter when it has to than the "Bonnie". Both feature disks all round, but the 300M's have more bite and feel, which inspires you to push it a little harder than you would its rival.

Slightly more expensive than the Pontiac, the Bonneville doesn't have quite the same following as yet either, but that can only be a matter of time. It's as well equipped as its competitor, arguably the more attractive and contemporary looking, and boasts more European levels of grip and handling than the ageing, but still very capable, Pontiac.

Pontiac BONNEVILLE SSEI

Inside Story

Introduced for 1992, the Bonneville is a member of GM's H-body full-size sedan family, sharing its inner structure with the Oldsmobile 88 and Buick Le Sabre. Unitary construction is employed, resulting in a stiff structure with few rattles. A separate subframe carries the engine and front suspension assembly, which consists of MacPherson struts and lower A-arms. Chapman struts are fitted at the back. Front and rear sway bars are standard on the SSEi.

POWER PACK

Powering all Bonnevilles is the 3800 series II V6. Based on a Buick design, it may seem old-fashioned, being a cast-iron pushrod unit with two valves per cylinder. However, with an Eaton supercharger, it gives the car levels of performance that rival many V8s. With the blower, plus sequential electronic fuel injection, electronic spark control and a coil for each cylinder, it pushes out 176kW (240bhp), and 379Nm (280lb-ft) of torque. This enables the Pontiac to reach 96km/h (60mph) in just 6.9 seconds.

Accommodation

The 300M boasts more interior space, but the Bonneville has a better driving position and more supportive front seats, making it much more comfortable on longer journeys.

Ride

Surprisingly, the new 300M has the harsher ride of the two. On rough surfaces, a substantial amount of harshness is transmitted into the cabin and through the steering. The Bonneville, by contrast, is much smoother over most surfaces and the driver is better isolated from road shocks.

Chrysler 300M

Inside Story

Like the Bonneville, the 300M is front drive with a unitary body and chassis. The latter has been considerably stiffened for 1999, with cross beams that connect the strong front suspension towers. Like the Pontiac, it has a separate front subframe cradle and MacPherson strut front suspension with Chapman struts at the rear. Larger strut pistons and revised suspension geometry on 1999 LH cars, plus a rear-suspension aluminum crossmember, result in excellent handling. Braking is by four-wheel disks.

P O W E R   P A C K

Although the lesser powered LH sedans have 3.2-liter V6s, as a performance option, the 300M packs a bigger and more powerful 3.5-liter unit. This is a new 24-valve, all-aluminum engine with dual overhead camshafts, as opposed to the Bonneville's overhead valve, single cam layout. The 3.2-liter produces 186kW (253bhp) and 345Nm (255lb-ft) of torque. This same engine is also found in 1999 Plymouth Prowlers.

Braking

Both cars employ four-wheel disks, though the Chrysler has vented items both front and rear, while the Pontiac has solid rear disks. For large American sedans, both cars are exceptional at braking, though the 300M has the slight edge here, stopping nearly 2.5m (8ft) shorter than the Bonneville from 96km/h (60mph) to rest, though from the cockpit the difference feels greater still.

Handling

Both cars employ virtually identical suspension set-ups, though the Chrysler feels the more nimble of the two, despite the fact that it is larger in every dimension. This is due to a more advanced suspension design and a stiffer structure. It also exhibits less body roll and the tires give more grip.

Chevrolet CAPRICE

Both cars of choice with law enforcement agencies, the late-model Ford Crown Victoria and Chevrolet Caprice are huge sedans that hark back to the golden age of motoring. But how do they fare against each other?

A sking America's law enforcers whether they prefer the Ford Crown Victoria or Chevrolet Caprice is like asking the average man on the street if they like Coke or Pepsi more. Each has become popular and their differences are so trivial, you really don't mind which is served up before you.

So, as America's second-most popular squad car, the Chevrolet Caprice is off to a good start, something it would also achieve on the road, where it proves quicker to 96km/h (60mph) and will hit 130km/h (80mph) virtually a full four seconds before the Ford. In fact, this surprising factory hot rod is rated to 225km/h (140mph) so is as quick as many

sports cars, making it an ideal police pursuit vehicle. Throw it around corners and dial in more speed and the Caprice exhibits less body roll than the Ford, as well as having greater feedback from the steering wheel.

And when the chase comes to an end, there's room to seat six adults as comfortably as they deserve in its spacious interior. In fact, the Caprice established such strong devotion from some of the many police departments that employed it, a cottage industry thrived in refurbishing them for continued police service when production finally came to an end. And you can't get a more glowing indictment than that.

CHEVROLET CAPRICE

Engine Capacity	5735cc (350cu in)
Weight	1855kg (4091lb)
Power	191kW (260bhp)
Torque	447.4Nm (330lb-ft) @ 3200 rpm
Price	$24,682
Acceleration:	
0–30mph (48km/h)	2.6 sec.
0–60mph (96km/h)	6.6 sec.
0–80mph (128km/h)	10.6 sec.
Standing ¼ mile (400m)	15.2 sec.
Maximum Speed	206km/h (128mph)

Ford CROWN VICTORIA

FORD CROWN VICTORIA

Engine Capacity	3572cc (218cu in)
Weight	1706kg (3761lb)
Power	140kW (190bhp)
Torque	352.5Nm (260lb-ft) @ 3250 rpm
Price	$23,250
Acceleration:	
0–30mph (48km/h)	3.1 sec.
0–60mph (96km/h)	6.1 sec.
0–80mph (128km/h)	14.5 sec.
Standing ¼ mile (400m)	16.4 sec.
Maximum Speed	225km/h (140mph)

There's an old saying: "If you want to know the time, ask a policeman." And if we were to modify that a little to ask a policeman or taxi driver for that matter, what is the most comfortable car for spending all day behind the wheel, what would do you think you'd hear? The most common response would be either the Ford Crown Victoria or Chevrolet Caprice.

Hardly surprising, as America's best-selling full-sized sedan, the Crown Victoria is the most popular "black and white" squad car or "yellow cab" there is. Both machines have tremendous amounts of interior space, for either paying customers or unwilling occupants, but the Ford has the greater rear legroom and feels the better built of the two.

For such a popular police interceptor the Ford is a remarkably huge and softly sprung car. Unlike the stiffer and more assured Chevy, it will soak up the deepest pot-holes and rough surfaces New York (or anywhere else) can offer and its passengers will barely notice a thing. Hit something too hard though and you'll find its "body-on-frame" construction makes repairing minor accidents so much easier too – no wonder the police love it.

Chevrolet CAPRICE

Inside Story

Like its Ford rival, the Caprice is essentially a new body on an old chassis, in this case a 1977-vintage platform. It also uses body-on-frame construction and retains a live rear axle. This one, however, has the LTZ package, which includes stiffer springs and shocks for a firmer ride, plus a larger front and rear anti-roll bar and bigger 235/70 VR15 radials mounted on cast-aluminum wheels. Like the Ford, the Chevy also comes with a four-speed automatic transmission, and front disk and rear drum brakes.

POWER PACK

From 1994, Caprice engine choices were a 4.3-liter (265cu in) V8 or an optional LT1 V8 motor which was also used in the Corvette and Camaro. In the Caprice, the LT1 has a cast-iron block and cylinder heads. Unlike the Ford engine, it retains a single camshaft and pushrods. Rated at 191kW (260bhp) and with 447Nm (330lb-ft) of torque, this engine boasts Multiport electronic fuel injection and makes the Caprice a star performer.

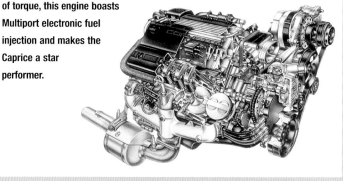

Road holding

With larger tires and bigger anti-roll bars, the Chevy takes to the pavement with more aplomb than the Ford. Around corners the Caprice also reveals less body roll and its firmer steering inspires greater driver confidence on twisty roads. The Crown Victoria is also quicker to lose adhesion at the limit.

Handling

Neither car is exactly nimble, but the Caprice, with its slightly firmer suspension, is more stable and exhibits less body roll than the Ford through sharp corners.

Ford CROWN VICTORIA

Inside Story

Although it received more contemporary styling for 1992, under the skin the basic Crown Victoria hardware dates back to 1979. The 289cm (114in) wheelbase separate steel chassis features an all-coil-sprung suspension – independent at the front but with a live axle at the rear. Front and rear anti-roll bars are used, although the chassis and springs are tuned for a soft ride rather than sporty handling. Brakes are front disks with drums at the rear.

POWER PACK

All Crown Victorias rely on Ford's 4.6-liter (281cu in) V8. Part of the 'modular' family of engines, which also includes a quad-cam, 5.4-liter (329cu in) and 6.8-liter (415cu in) V10, the 4.6 is of cast-iron construction with a single overhead camshaft for each cylinder bank. Like most modern engines, it has electronic spark control, and a sequential electronic fuel-injection system feeds fuel to each of the cylinders. It is rated at 140kW (190bhp) in base form.

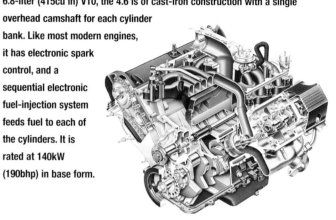

Accommodation

Both cars offer tremendous interior space, able to seat six adults in comfort. The Ford, however, seems to make better use of this space, offering more legroom at the rear. Its interior also seems to be of better quality, with the controls more logically placed.

Ride

Aimed at buyers of traditional American sedans, both of these behemoths have been tuned to give a pillow-soft ride. The Chevy, with its stiffer springs and shock valving, delivers a more taut ride over rough pavement. The Ford is much smoother and is more effective at isolating road noise and vibration.

Mercedes-Benz SLK

The open sports car revival of the late 1990s produced fierce competition, pitching Mercedes' lightweight SLK against Porsche's new Boxster. Could the Mercedes' supercharged four hold its own against Porsche's flat-six Boxster?

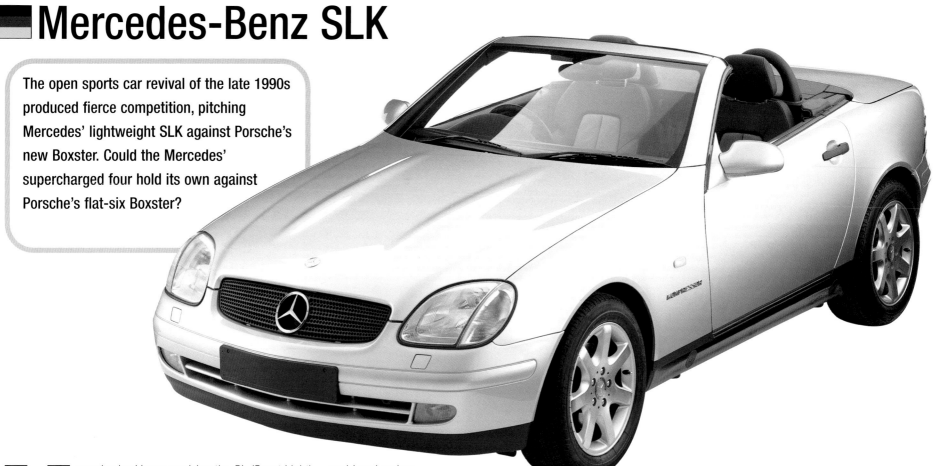

Mercedes had been applying the SL (Sport Light) tag to some of its sportier models for many years, but the SLK (with K standing for Kompressor – its supercharger) was the first model to fully deserve the name in recent times.

More refined and comfortable than the Boxster, theses two cars vie for sales in today's highly competitive sports-car market, but the SLK offers the best of both worlds. One minute it's a cosy tin-top, the next – and at the push of a button – its clever metal roof folds out of the way and you're driving a rapid and capable, supercharged two-seat roadster. In fact, its mechanical metal roof is one of the best in the world and makes for easier living in wetter countries. Truly then, a sports car for all seasons.

Not for nothing has the SLK become one of Mercedes-Benz's best-selling roadsters of all time. It's small, light, and incredibly fast and while both cars are almost perfectly matched in terms of acceleration and top speed, the SLK has a more solid, chunky, high-quality feel as it floats over bumps and uneven surfaces in the road as though it were a much larger car. If ever a two-seater sports car felt like it was hewn from a solid metal billet it's the tough little SLK.

MERCEDES-BENZ SLK

Engine Capacity	2295cc (140cu in)
Weight	872kg (1922lb)
Power	142kW (193bhp)
Torque	279.3Nm (206lb-ft) @ 2,500 rpm
Price	$39,700
Acceleration:	
0–30mph (48km/h)	2.9 sec.
0–60mph (96km/h)	8.1 sec.
0–125mph (200km/h)	40.0 sec.
Standing ¼ mile (400m)	15.5 sec.
Maximum Speed	230km/h (143mph)

Porsche BOXSTER

PORSCHE BOXTER

Engine Capacity	2480cc (151cl)
Weight	1252kg (2761lb)
Power	150kW (204bhp)
Torque	245.4Nm (181lb-ft) @ 4500 rpm
Price	$30,980

Acceleration:

0–30mph (48km/h)	2.6 sec.
0–60mph (96km/h)	6.9 sec.
0–125mph (200km/h)	35.5 sec.
Standing ¼ mile (400m)	14.8 sec.
Maximum Speed	240km/h (149mph)

There have been many 'entry-level' Porsches over the years, but it was the Boxster that really caught on and gave the German manufacturer the shot in the arm it so desperately needed. Having relied on the 911 to keep the factory afloat for so long, it seems odd to build a car that is visually so similar. However, it proved to be a very smart move as it offered virtually the same looks and almost the same performance as its big brother, but with none of its vices and for a good deal less cash.

Unlike the rear-engined 911 and traditional front-engined SLK, the Boxster feels like it's glued to the road and far less likely to break away at speed. With its compact mid-mounted engine the Porsche is almost perfectly balanced and feels more agile and eager to please than the SLK. And there's a real difference under normal conditions as well, because the Mercedes seems almost too refined and sedan-like, compared to the Porsche, which is sharper and rawer, yet still comfortable enough to use every day if you wish.

It might be the Porsche for the masses, but the Boxster is still a real driver's car – even more so than the SLK. Destined to be Porsche's bestseller, it's more involving to drive, and its badge has slightly more kudos too.

Mercedes-Benz SLK

Inside Story

Its conventional layout sees the four-cylinder engine mounted at the front driving the rear wheels in the traditional way. Structure is a steel monocoque, although Mercedes uses weight-saving magnesium in some areas, such as the bulkhead behind the trunk and the cam cover, the SLK is still quite heavy. Clever five-link rear suspension is used along with double-wishbone front suspension. Mercedes offers a five-speed manual or automatic transmission.

POWER PACK

The twin-cam, four-cylinder engine has an alloy block and head and four valves per cylinder. A slightly oversquare design gives a displacement of 2295cc (140cu in). Power output from 2.3 liters is an excellent 141kW (193bhp) thanks to the intercooled mechanically-driven super-charger, which also helps it produce an impressive amount of torque. Its maximum 279Nm (206lb-ft) is also produced at an accessible 2500 rpm, another feature of supercharging. At 8.8:1, the compression ratio is surprisingly high for a supercharged engine.

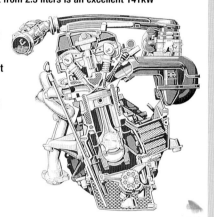

Ride

The worse the road gets, the more impressive the SLK becomes. It offers comfort, but seems too sedan-like. The Porsche's ride is comfortable, too but doesn't compromise the Boxster's sporty feel.

Braking

Porsche claim to give their cars the world's best brakes. The lighter Boxster should have the edge in theory, but it's the SLK that stops more quickly, coming to a stop in a couple of yards before the Boxster with cold brakes, although the margin is less when the brakes are steaming hot.

Porsche BOXSTER

Inside Story

Boxster's steel monocoque has the engine mounted behind the cockpit and ahead of the rear wheels instead of at the back like the 911. The flat-six engine is mated to a five-speed manual or five-speed semi-automatic Tiptronic transmission. Another contrast to the 911 sees MacPherson strut suspension used at the front and rear for packaging reasons, not because the new 911's wishbone rear suspension isn't better. In theory, the struts may be inferior, but in practice, they work very well.

P O W E R   P A C K

The Boxster is mid-engined and water- rather than air-cooled, because it's harder to get air flow around a mid-mounted engine and to make it quieter as it's closer to the occupants. Despite its big bore and short stroke (8.5 x 7cm/ 3.38 inch x 2.83 inch) the 24-valve, quad-cam design is still wide enough to have an effect on the car's overall width, but it's dry sumped to make it low. Without a turbo or supercharger, maximum torque of 245Nm (181lb-ft) is produced at a high 4500 rpm.

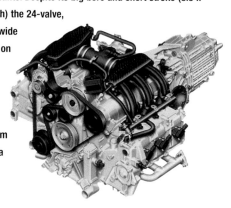

Road holding

The SLK comes into its own on rough surfaces when the suspension refuses to be thrown off-line by bumps. Mid-engined Boxster grips tenaciously and its strut suspension soaks up bumps without deflecting the car's path, giving it the edge over the SLK.

Performance

Porsche's new engine is sluggish at low rpm but really picks up higher in the range. It gives the Boxster a clear performance advantage over the decently-quick supercharged SLK.

Glossary of Technical Terms

A

A-pillar Angled roof supports each side of the front windscreen

ABS Anti-lock braking system

Acceleration Rate of change of velocity, usually expressed as a measure of time over a given distance such as a quarter of a mile, or from rest to a given speed, such as 0–60mph

Aerodynamic drag Wind resistance, expressed as a coefficient of drag (Cd); the more streamlined a vehicle, the lower the figure

Aftermarket Accessory fitted to a vehicle after purchase, not always offered by the manufacturer

Air-cooled engine Where ambient air is used to cool the engine, by passing directly over fins on the cylinders and cylinder head

Air dam Device at the front of a car to reduce air flow underneath the vehicle and thus reduce lift at high speeds

Aluminium block Engine cylinder block cast from aluminum, usually with cast iron sleeves or liners for the cylinder bores

Anti-roll bar Transverse rod between left and right suspension at front or rear to reduce body roll

B

B-pillar roof and door frame support behind the driver

bhp Brake horse power, 1 bhp = raising 550 foot-pounds per second; 1 bhp = torque x rpm/5252 with torque measured in foot-pounds

Blown engine or "blower" Engine fitted with a system of forced air induction such as a supercharger or turbocharger

Bucket seat Seat with added support in leg and shoulder area to secure the driver while cornering, used in rally sport

C

C-pillar Side pillar to the rear of the rear seats supporting the roof

Camshaft Engine component which controls the opening and closing of valves via lobes, either directly or indirectly

Carburetor Device for vaporizing fuel and mixing it with air in an exact ratio ready for combustion, via the inlet manifold

Chassis Component to which body, engine, gearbox and suspension are attached

Close ratio Gearbox with closely spaced ratios, used in competition

Clutch Device for controlling the transmission of power from the engine to the gearbox, usually by means of friction materials

Coil spring Helical steel alloy rod used for vehicle suspension

Column change Gearchange lever mounted on the steering column

Con rod Connecting rod that links the piston and the crankshaft, the little end connecting to the piston and the big end connecting to the crankshaft

Cylinder chamber in which piston travels, usually cylindrical in shape

Cylinder head Component which carries the sparkplugs, valves, and sometimes camshafts

D

Differential Arrangement of gears in the drive axle which allows the drive wheel on the outside of a bend to travel faster than the one on the inside

Disc brake System of braking by which friction pads are pressed against a flat, circular metal surface

Double wishbone Method of suspension where each wheel is supported by an upper and lower pivoting triangular framework

Downdraft carburettor Carburetor with a vertical barrel

Driveshaft Shaft that transmits drive from the differential to the wheel, especially on front wheel drive cars with independent rear suspension

Drivetrain Entire power transmission system from the engine's pistons to its tyres

Dry sump Where lubricating oil is contained in a separate reservoir rather than being held in the crankcase; often used in competition to prevent oil surge/starvation

E

Exhaust Device, usually of metal pipe construction, to conduct spent combustion gases away from the engine

F

Fascia A car's dashboard or instrument panel

Flathead Style of engine where the valves are mounted in the cylinder block, and the cylinder head has a flat surface

Flat twin/flat four Boxer engine configuration where cylinders are horizontally opposed to each other, such as in the VW Beetle

Floorpan Structural floor to a car, part of the chassis

Fluid clutch Clutch using a fluid coupling, flywheel, or torque converter

Forced induction Engine using a turbocharger or supercharger to pressurize the induction system to force air and hence more fuel, giving more power

Fuel injection Direct metered injection of fuel into the combustion cycle by mechanical or electro-mechanical means, first devised in 1902

G

Gearbox Component of the transmission system that houses a number of gears of different ratios that can be selected either automatically or manually by the driver. Different gears are selected to suit a variety of road speeds throughout the engine's rev range

Gear ratio The revolutions of a driving gear required to turn the driven gear through one revolution, calculated by the number of teeth on the driven gear divided by the number of teeth on the driving gear

Grand tourer Term originally used to describe an open-top luxury car, now typically a high performance coupé

Grill Metal or plastic protection for the radiator, often adopting a particular style or design of an individual manufacturer to make their car recognizable

GT Gran Turismo; Italian term used to describe a high performance luxury sports car or coupé

Gullwing Doors that open in a vertical arc, usually hinged along the centre of the roofline

H

H-pattern Conventional gear selection layout where first and third gear are furthest from the driver and second and fourth are nearest

Helical gears Gear wheel with its teeth set oblique to the gear axis which mates with another shaft with its teeth at the same angle

Hemi engine An engine with a hemispherical combustion chamber

Hydrolastic suspension System of suspension where

compressible fluids act as springs, with interconnections between wheels to aid levelling

I

Independent suspension System of suspension where all wheels move up and down independently of each other, thus having no effect on the other wheels and aiding stability

Intercooler Device to cool supercharged or turbocharged air before it enters the engine to increase density and power

K

Kamm tail Type of rear body design developed by W. Kamm, where the rear end of the car tapers sharply over the rear window and is then cut vertically to improve aerodynamics

L

Ladder frame Tradition form of chassis with two constructional rails running front to rear with lateral members adding rigidity

Limited slip differential Device to control the difference in speed between left and right driveshafts so both wheels turn at similar speeds. Fitted to reduce the likelihood of wheelspinning on slippery surfaces

Live axle Axle assembly patented by Louis Renault in 1899. The axle contains shafts which drive the wheels

M

Manifold Pipe system used for gathering or dispersal of gas or liquids

Mid-engine Vehicle with its engine mounted just behind the driver and significantly ahead of the rear axle to provide even weight distribution, thus giving the car better handling characteristics

Monobloc An engine with all its cylinders cast in one piece

Monocoque Body design where the bodyshell carries the structural strength without conventional chassis rails (see "unitary construction")

O

Overdrive Additional higher ratio gear(s), usually on the third or fourth gear selected automatically by the driver

R

Rack and pinion System of gearing typically used in a steering box with a toothed rail driven laterally by a pinion on the end of the steering column

Radiator Device for dissipating heat, generally from the engine coolant

Rocker arms Pivoting arm translating rotational movement of the camshaft into linear movement of the valves

Roll bar Strong, usually curved bar either internally or eternally across a vehicle's roof then secured to the floor or chassis to provide protection in the event of the car turning over. Used on some open-top sportcars

Running gear General description of a vehicle's underbody mechanicals, including the suspension, steering, brakes, and drivetrain

S

Semi-elliptic spring Leaf spring suspension used on the rear axle of older cars in which the spring conforms to a specific mathematical shape

Semi-independent suspension System on a front-wheel drive car where the wheels are located by trailing links and a torsioned crossmember

Sequential gearbox Gear selection layout in which the selection is made by a linear movement rather than in the conventional H-pattern, used on some sportscars and rally cars

Servo assistance Servo powered by a vacuum, air, hydraulics, or electrically to aid the driver to give a powerful output from minimal input. Typically used on brakes, steering and clutch

Shock absorber Hydraulic device, part of the suspension system typically mounted between the wheel and the chassis to prevent unwanted movement, to increase safety and aid comfort. More correctly known as "damper"

Spark plug Device for igniting combustion gases via the arcing of current between two electrodes

"Split driveline" layout An extra set of epicyclic gears to provide a closer interval between the standard set of ratios, so an eight speed gearbox will actually have 16 gears

Spoiler Device fitted to the front of the car, low to the ground, to reduce air flow under the car and increase down-force, thus improving roadholding at higher speeds

Straight 6, 8 An engine with six or eight cylinders in a single row

Supercharger Mechanically-driven air pump used to force air into the combustion cycle, improving performance

Synchromesh Automatic synchronization using cone clutches to speed up or slow down the input shaft to smoothly engage gear, first introduced by Cadillac in 1928

T

Tachometer device for measuring rotational speed (revs per minute, rpm) of an engine

Torque The rotational twisting force exerted by the crankshaft

Traction control Electronic system of controlling the amount of power to a given wheel to reduce wheelspin

Transmission General term for the final drive, clutch and gearbox.

Transverse engine Engine type where the crankshaft lies parallel to the axle

Turbocharger Air pump for use in forced induction engines. Similar to a supercharger but driven at very high speed by exhaust gases, rather than mechanically to increase power output

U

Unibody Monocoque construction in which the floorpan, chassis and body are welded together to form one single structure

Unitary construction Monocoque bodyshell structurally rigid enough not to require a separate chassis

Unit construction Engine in which the powerplant and transmission are together as one, integrated unit

V

Venturi principle Basis upon which carburetors work: gas flowing through a narrow opening creates a partial vacuum

W

Wheelbase The measured distance between the front and rear wheel spindles

Index

Index